CALLED TO TEACH

A Biblical Challenge To Renounce Intellectual Idolatry And Dedicate
Ourselves To Spiritual Discipleship On Christian School Campuses

KENNETH O. GANGEL, PH.D.

Published By
ASSOCIATION OF CHRISTIAN SCHOOLS INTERNATIONAL
P.O. Box 35097 • Colorado Springs • Colorado 80935

TABLE OF CONTENTS

AUTHOR'S INTRODUCTION

For thirty-five years I have been involved in Christian higher education, eighteen at the undergraduate level and seventeen at the graduate. All during those three-and-a-half decades, I have also served Christian education at elementary and secondary levels, and of course, church education. The central word in all that ministry is millennia old—teaching.

And that is the theme of this book. To be sure, Christian education deals with more than classroom performance. But if that fails, we have nothing to offer a needy society looking to our schools for a timeless yet fresh approach to learning and living.

My long tenure in the field, coupled with annual contact with thousands of teachers from the seminary faculty I lead to conferees at ACSI conventions, clearly colors this book. Certain themes appear with regularity throughout its chapters: Christian teaching as a vocation, the centrality of Scripture in our curricula, society's failure to reward its teachers, the practice and extension of integration on Christian campuses, and several others.

Nor are the chapter titles and texts original. Veteran ACSI convention attendees will recognize them from the past eighteen years. In plenary sessions each year, I have attempted to address and apply the mottoes selected by headquarters staff. Greatly revised and updated, those addresses form the chapters of this book.

So much of what we do is pragmatic, the necessary preoccupation with how—lesson plans, testing and grading, discipline, parental relations, and the seemingly endless paperwork of our profession. Though this books deals with some of these, its greater purpose centers on the what and the why of Christian teaching.

Beyond the daily duty, behind the weekly work, behind the monthly mundane, lies the meaning of what we do. I have attempted in these chapters to allow the warming and clarifying spotlight of God's Word to shine upon our heavenly calling, to elevate it, to dignify it, and to demonstrate its crucial importance. In the process, I pray His Holy Spirit will challenge, convict, encourage, affirm and strengthen all those special and wonderful people He has "called to teach."

One further thought. Books like this are rarely the product of one person's efforts. Word of appreciation are due two of my assistants: Christy Sullivan for research and editing and Ginny Murray for manuscript preparation. So much of what I do would be impossible without them.

Kenneth O. Gangel, Ph.D.
Dallas, Texas

DEDICATION

To all Christian school teachers around the world,
pioneers as well as rookies, from pre-K to physics, may
these chapters affirm and enhance your call to teach.

CHAPTER ONE

PREPARED UNTO EVERY GOOD WORK

vessel unto honour, sancti
and meet for the master's use,
3.1. *and* prepared unto every good
work.
22 Flee also youthful lusts:
follow righteousness, faith

2 Timothy 2:14-21

Words! How many do you say each day? How do they affect your hearers? We all know the familiar school yard rhyme, "Sticks and stones will break my bones, but words will never hurt me." Children use that phrase as a defense from unfair taunts and painful comments from their peers. Say it bravely they might, but they know inside that it carries no truth. Cutting and nasty words do hurt; unkind comments on appearance or physical characteristics may produce lifelong scars; deliberate put-downs may drive a young person to desperate insecurities or deep depressions.

Words such as marriage vows bind people together for life; words consisting of hateful accusations can split people apart just as irrevocably. Alphabets, vocabulary, grammar, order lie at the foundation of our communion with one another. Words give us stories, the "once upon a times . . ." that transport us to worlds we may never actually visit with our bodies, but can enjoy with our minds. Words provide a means for the powerful metaphorical imagery of good poetry that permits a short phrase to draw a whole mental picture. When we read, "For our God is a consuming fire . . ." or "I am the Good Shepherd" we know far more than just these simple phrases would suggest on the surface.

At the very beginning of our created history we see the power of the spoken word as God said, "Let there be light." Adam showed dominion over nature when by the spoken word he named the animals. And then there is the Word, the Book of Life, the Bible given to us that we might have a glimpse of the glory of God. What a privilege we have as Christian educators that the centrality of our teaching focuses on this revelation!

What encompasses the boundaries of the proper use of words and the Word? What preparation should we find necessary in order to minister as Christian educators who teach to change lives, not just to transmit words?

Let's dip into a passage of Scripture which will help us set those boundaries as we work at winning a war of words and preparing for a purity of purpose.

WINNING THE WAR OF WORDS

Keep reminding them of these things. Warn them before God against quarreling about words; it is of no value, and only ruins those who listen. Do your best to present yourself to God as one approved, a workman who does not need to be ashamed and who correctly handles the word of truth. Avoid godless chatter, because those who indulge in it will become more and more ungodly. Their teaching will spread like gangrene. Among them are Hymenaeus and Philetus, who have wandered away from the truth. They say that the resurrection has already taken place, and they destroy the faith of some. Nevertheless, God's solid foundation stands firm, sealed with this inscription: "The Lord knows those who are his," and, "Everyone who confesses the name of the Lord must turn away from wickedness." (2 Timothy 2:14–19)

> "We will be God's mouthpieces if we avoid quarreling, gossip and false doctrine and focus ourselves and our students on the solid foundation of God's truth."

Words! Again I ask, "How many do you say each day?" Probably more if you are a kindergarten teacher than if you preside over a chemistry lab, but words make up the very stuff of our profession. Carpenters work with wood; artists work with paint; musicians work with notes; we work with words. But the old cliché "winning the war of words" does not take its traditional meaning in this paragraph of God's Word. Here the way up is down and the one who shouts louder or talks longer wins neither in nor out of the classroom. Five kinds of words emerge in our passage.

Quarreling Words

How could a Bible passage be more clear? Christian teachers and administrators who quarrel about words simply waste their time and ruin any who listen to them. The Greek word translated "quarreling about words" appears only here in the New Testament. The word "ruin" is literally "catastrophe," again a word found only here in the entire New Testament. A Christian school campus ought to be like the idyllic homestead in the old country song "Home on the Range": "where never is heard a discouraging word and the skies are not cloudy all day."

A hopeless ideal? Of course. But the more we work to delete quarreling from our relationships with peers, supervisors and students, the more God will use our words to prepare people to do any good work.

Before we leave verse 14, however, let's note that we have begun in the middle of a chapter and the words "these things" refer back to the first thirteen verses. Christian teachers constantly remind students of the things which God has said, especially the truth of sound doctrine and, in the immediate context, the reality of the resurrection of Jesus Christ. What a great sentence appears at the end of verse 9: "But God's Word is not chained." Some have suggested verses 11 through 13 form an early Christian hymn reminding believers that any kind of suffering for Christ will be followed by glory.

THE YEAR 1978

- ACSI was formed as a result of a merger of the National Christian School Education Association (NCSEA), the Western Association of Christian Schools (WACS), and the Ohio Association of Christian Schools (OACS). Dr. Paul Kienel, of WACS, was appointed to serve as Executive Director. Dr. Roy Lowrie, Jr., served part-time as President. The first year's membership was 1,051 schools with a combined student enrollment of 185,687.

- The first ACSI Executive Staff and Executive Board meetings were held on the campus of Grace College and Seminary in Winona Lake, Indiana, on July 21.

REFLECTING ON THE HISTORY OF ACSI

Bible Words

Do your best to present yourself to God as one approved, a workman who does not need to be ashamed and who correctly handles the word of truth. (2 Timothy 2:15)

Here we find one of the most familiar verses of the entire Bible. The familiar term "study" appears in the New International Version as "do your best." Other possible translations include "make haste" or "be zealous." The point is that Christian teachers make every effort to stand before God as unashamed workers *who can correctly handle the Word of Truth.* In secular Greek literature this last phrase referred to cutting a road across the country much in the way a forester might clear the brush from a hiking path or even a fire lane.

Christian teachers handle Bible words in such a way that they chop down trees, push aside fallen debris, and keep clear for future passage the way their students ought to walk. Notice that we do this not by the way we handle math or science, as important as our academic disciplines are. We do it by the way we handle God's Word in relationship to those disciplines, a practice we have commonly called *integration*. When it comes to the issue of handling the Bible in our classrooms, we want to be approved workers who have no reason whatsoever to be ashamed.

Godless Words

Avoid godless chatter, because those who indulge in it will become more and more ungodly. (2 Timothy 2:16)

What a challenge for those of us who inhabit Christian classrooms. How easy to substitute our own interpretations—our little pet views on certain verses or theological ideas—for a broad understanding of God's truth. Godless chatter does not necessarily refer specifically to gossip but rather simply empty sounds, the same warning Timothy received at the end of the first letter (1 Timothy 6:20).

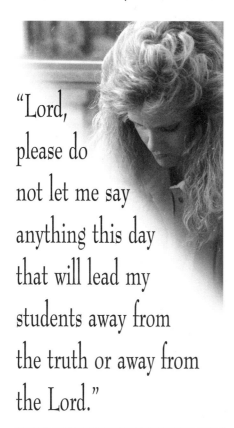

"Lord, please do not let me say anything this day that will lead my students away from the truth or away from the Lord."

We do not talk here about complaints concerning the quality of coffee in the faculty lounge. Rather the spotlight falls upon words that hurt other people because they are untrue, unhelpful or frivolous. Small wonder James warned his readers at the beginning of chapter three that not many of them should be teachers because extensive tongue use creates greater responsibility.

Heresy Words

Their teaching will spread like gangrene. Among them are Hymenaeus and Philetus, who have wandered away from the truth. They say that the resurrection has already taken place, and they destroy the faith of some. (2 Timothy 2:17–18)

Here Paul goes back to his discussion of the Resurrection in earlier parts of the chapter and names two false teachers, Hymenaeus and Philetus, who have wandered away from the truth. The Bible uses a graphic simile here, reminding us that false teaching spreads like gangrene. This word appears only here in the New Testament though commonly used by medical writers in the first century to describe a kind of sore that eats into the flesh. We don't know who these two men were, nor is that important to our purpose. We do know that people who do not watch their words can subvert the faith of others. If true about adults among other adults, how frighteningly true must it be of adults who hold awesome power over the minds of children in a classroom. Our morning prayers ought always to include some form of the following petition: "Lord, please do not let me say anything this day that will lead my students away from the truth or away from the Lord."

God's Words

Nevertheless, God's solid foundation stands firm, sealed with this inscription: "The Lord knows those who are his," and, "Everyone who confesses the name of the Lord must turn away from wickedness." (2 Timothy 2:19)

Despite the heresies that swirl around us, despite the careless mischievous use of words, God's Word stands firm. These quotes sound like mottoes of effective Christian schools: "The Lord knows those who are his" and "Everyone who confesses the name of the Lord must turn away from wickedness." Not a bad idea for two sides of a souvenir coin. The first comes from Numbers 16:5 and the second, though not exactly a quotation, seems related to phraseology in the same chapter.

God's solid foundation stands firm. Yet these are not days in which solid foundations can easily be found. Family fragmentation continues at an alarming rate and no reasons for hope seem available. In America over 2.3 million people live together without a marriage bond and 700,000 of those households have children. In addition, 92,000 domiciles shared by gay or lesbian couples house children.[1]

We have seen a significant decline in work ethic as one of the long-term trends affecting the United States. Focus has shifted from remuneration (salary and benefits) to the advantage work provides to the worker. That shift reflects the high priority of time over money as the number one currency of the society. Another demonstration, termed "cocooning" in the last decade, indicates the return to the home as the center of all life's activities and relationships, from running a telemarketing program for employment to playing Trivial Pursuit or Pictionary on Friday night.

"In 1978 I was a first-year teacher, attending my first ACSI teacher convention, when I heard this message by Dr. Gangel. It was during that conference that I realized that my teaching ministry extended far beyond my own classroom."

~ Sandra, Texas

Barna cites a trend toward different spouses for different eras of life claiming, "By 2000, Americans will generally believe that a life spent with the same partner is both unusual and unnecessary. We will continue our current moral transition by accepting sexual relationships with one person at a time—'serial monogamy'—to be the civilized and moral way to behave. But we will not consider it at all unusual to be married two or three times during the course of life."[2] In such an environment Christian teachers cling to God's words, planting their pedagogical feet on His solid, firm foundation.

PREPARING FOR PURITY OF PURPOSE

In a large house there are articles not only of gold and silver, but also of wood and clay; some are for noble purposes and some for ignoble. If a man cleanses himself from the latter, he will be an instrument for noble purposes, made holy, useful to the Master and prepared to do any good work. (2 Timothy 2:20–21)

The tragedy of all this family breakdown described in the previous paragraphs magnifies its effect in the lives of children. In 1988, 12.5 million U.S. children lived in poverty. Between 6.6 and 10.6 million kids under twelve go hungry every day in America. Some studies claim this country contains more than 100,000 homeless children.[3]

Of course, compared to the world scale, our problem seems small. Over 14 million under the age of five die each year from infection and malnutrition and at least 100 million children of primary school age, worldwide, will never enter a classroom.[4] To put that in perspective, if one hundred jumbo jets—each loaded with infants and children—crashed every day for ten years, that would be equivalent to the number of children dying from malnutrition and infection. Think about that in light of the income figures of politicians, professional athletes and punk rock musicians. I do not object simply to high incomes, but rather to the way society values the wrong things when setting income levels.

What does the American family look like? According to George Barna, "The average American family in 1990 consisted of a married couple with one child, in which both parents are employed. At least one of the parents is likely to have been divorced, or will be divorced."[5]

The size of the average family is 3.7 and the average household, 2.64. People marry later, have children later, have fewer children, and although one cannot compare infant survival rates with numbers of forty or fifty years ago, it is rather shocking to discover that the United States ranks twentieth in the world in that statistic.[6]

What may we expect from the society that nourishes this family? North American twenty-first century society will be older and dominated by minorities. The migration from the rust belt to the sun belt will continue in a society which opposes Christian values and ideals while

> "We will be God's vessels if we cleanse ourselves from inappropriate purposes—self-advancement, manipulation, unclean behavior—and accept whatever task God has given us to achieve His goals in our schools."

experiencing such painful effects as the breakdown of family, school system and other societal structures. All this takes place against the now familiar backdrop of terrorism, pollution, drug abuse and crime. Leith Anderson argues that the church of present and future decades is one marked by globalization, urbanization and democratization.[7]

Major national trends mark the culture in which we teach, including significant demographics. The 1990 census showed that America contains approximately 250 million people. "That is 23 million more people than in 1980, representing a 10 percent increase."[8] Demographers use the term "baby boomers" to describe 76 million Americans born between 1946 and 1964 with 1957 the peak year.

The first baby boomers turn fifty in the middle of this decade and experts expect that as many as one million boomers will reach the age of one hundred. American baby boomers and their children now comprise about half the U.S. population. They control an estimated 55 percent of consumer spending, head roughly 44 percent of households, and make up most of the electorate.[9] They are a true global village generation marked by low loyalty to almost anything, high expectations from almost everyone and a nagging unpredictability with respect to liberal or conservative orientation in politics or religion.

In such a context God has raised up a community of Christians who have been called to teach. In the passage before us we have already learned how these teachers can win the war of words. Now Paul switches the metaphor from words to pots and bowls in order to emphasize purity of purpose.

Types of Dishes

The word translated "articles" simply means jars or dishes. Most important are the gold ones used for special guests and festive occasions. The second category of silver is linked with the gold in worth of use but obviously of slightly lesser value. One cannot run a household merely with gold and silver dishes; there must be mixing bowls and cooking pots, vessels made of wood and clay.

Some would make a special distinction here between the two types of dishes in the latter part of verse 20, saying that gold and silver dishes serve noble purposes and wood and clay vessels, ignoble. But that doesn't fit the metaphor (as we have already noted), nor does it fit Paul's testimony in 2 Corinthians 4:7 where he reminds us that "we have this treasure in jars of clay to show that this all-surpassing power is from God and not from us."

My fellow teachers, I offer an alternative interpretation of the passage which affirms the value of all vessels, even those which do not seem gold and silver to the public eye. Headmasters and board chairpersons appear gold and silver because of their titles, roles and visibility. But meals, however festive, cannot be served on gold dishes unless the food has been prepared in clay pots first. Our movement survives and thrives because thousands of wood and clay vessels wipe runny noses, sweep up littered floors after school, agonize endlessly over unbalanced school budgets and carry out scores of tasks back in the kitchen so we can serve the guests when they come. Construction of the vessel is not the issue; its utility and condition create value.

Condition of the Dishes

Finally we come to our key verse, though the phrase which forms the title falls only at the end. Are you a vessel of gold? Then by all means be clean. Are you a vessel of wood or clay? The same rule applies. Not that the gold and silver must separate themselves from the wood and clay, but rather that those who would be used for noble purposes must separate themselves from ignoble purposes. Christian teachers whom God uses must be "made holy, useful to the Master, and prepared to do any good work." Those teachers can then be used to prepare their students to do any good work.

Another chapter in this book deals with the rest of 2 Timothy 2, but for now we want to focus on what we have learned just in these two paragraphs. We will be God's mouthpieces if we avoid quarreling, gossip and false doctrine and focus ourselves and our students on the solid foundation of God's truth. We will be God's vessels if we cleanse ourselves from inappropriate purposes—self-advancement, manipulation, unclean behavior—and accept whatever task God has given us to achieve His goals in our schools.

ENDNOTES

1. Kim Painter, "Unmarried—With Children," *USA Today* (13 May 1988).
2. George Barna, *The Frog in the Kettle* (Ventura, Calif.: Regal Books, 1990), 72.
3. Kim A. Lawton, "The World's Most Venerable," *Christianity Today* (19 November 1990): 48.
4. Ibid.
5. Barna, *Frog*, 66.
6. Ibid., 187
7. Leith Anderson, *Dying for Change* (Minneapolis: Bethany House, 1990), 24.
8. Barna, *Frog*, 185.
9. Gary R. Collins and Timothy E. Clinton, *Baby Boomer Blues* (Dallas: Word Publishing, 1992).

CHAPTER TWO

1979

IN ALL THY WAYS ACKNOWLEDGE HIM

thine heart; and lea...
unto thine own understanding...
6 In all thy ways acknowledge him, and he shall direct
thy paths.
7 Be not wise in thine own...
...the LORD, and...

Proverbs 3:1-12

Christian and non-Christian alike, North Americans love mottoes. One single cultural phenomenon, the slogan T-shirt, reveals our romance with short pithy statements. In some cases we wear them to describe the owner's point of view or perhaps to be rebellious, humorous or just chic. In addition to T-shirts, we have bumper stickers and billboards all offering one-liners to attract attention and make a point. Christians especially seem to value wall plaques with lines such as "God is the Head of this Household" or "Prayer Changes Things." All of which is completely harmless and perhaps even beneficial unless we begin thinking that mottoes—or even proverbs from the Bible—represent promises of God.

Neither a promise nor a precept, a proverb is simply a short poignant phrase whose meaning can apply in many situations. Proverbs offer lessons by reflecting on the way things and people relate to right values and right conduct. We hardly compromise the authority and inerrancy of the book by remembering that its literary style is neither historical (like much of the Old Testament and Acts) nor didactic (like the Pauline epistles). It calls readers to fear God and to behave in ways that please Him. The theme before us in this chapter, drawn from verse 6, crouches in a context admonishing us to follow the way of wisdom in relationships with God and other people.

> "Neither a promise nor a precept, a proverb is simply a short poignant phrase whose meaning can apply in many situations."

One finds it difficult to imagine a Christian school teacher or administrator who does not affirm an eagerness to acknowledge God in all life's ways. But what exactly does that mean? What kinds of things must you and I remember in order to activate the lessons of this passage? Perhaps a series of negative imperatives will help plant this theme in our hearts and classrooms.

DON'T FORGET MY TEACHING

My son, do not forget my teaching,
but keep my commands in your heart,
for they will prolong your life many years
and bring you prosperity.
(Proverbs 3:1–2)

Why not start off a class next week with that kind of guarantee? Imagine yourself telling a homeroom full of students that if they will remember and activate what you have taught them, their lives will be prolonged and full of prosperity.

Obviously, the father/son relationship so common in Proverbs applies here. We should not be surprised to find Solomon, of all people, extolling wisdom and affirming that the practice of righteousness, as he conveyed it to his children, could produce long life and prosperity. We find it relatively easy to believe that children who obey godly parents will live better lives than those who do not. Likewise, students who ingest and implement what they learn in a Christian school should enjoy happier lives before God than those who had no such privilege, or those who rebel against it.

But unless we remember that this is a proverb not a promise, we could easily fall victim to what has been called in recent years "prosperity gospel." Yes, quite often the righteous are prosperous and happy (Proverbs 12:21), but the Bible teaches that wicked people also enjoy strength and prosperity (Psalm 73:3, 12).

Paul spends a great deal of time in 2 Corinthians explaining that suffering rather than prosperity marked his life and ministry. The first part of our passage tells us that we as Christian teachers share responsibility with parents in creating a value system which gives young people the opportunity to live rich and fruitful lives before God.

William Willimon, dean of the chapel at Duke University, writes about his "conversion" to Christian Education:

Increasing numbers of Christians suspect that the public schools' pride in liberating students from parental values, tradition, community and religion has only rendered young people more subservient to the dominant values of the State. Wolterstorff envisions new schools as "distinct sub-communities in which the conditions are still present for cultivation of ethical sensitivity and developing moral character."[1]

Yes, we want moral character well established in our students—but we also want it in their parents. How many tears, how much energy have teachers expended over some students while watching careless parents undo what we have so carefully crafted in the classroom.

Perhaps my point focuses primarily on our willingness to understand why parents hesitate to move ahead on our suggestions. Obviously, we dare never forget God's order of priority and our servant role in the wider scheme of things. Ultimately the *parent* must say, "Do not forget my teaching." Somehow God must give us both grace and persistence in encouraging our students to remember the truth and faith we have taught them and in helping parents assume their appropriate Biblical roles.

DON'T FORGET TO BE LOVING AND FAITHFUL

> Let love and faithfulness never leave you;
>   bind them around your neck,
>   write them on the tablet of your heart.
> Then you will win favor and a good name
>   in the sight of God and man.
> (Proverbs 3:3–4)

Here again we have an admonition followed by a reward. Love and faithfulness served as two basic covenant terms in ancient Israel. The word for "love" here refers to the kind of obligations one incurs in a relationship. "Faithfulness" reflects precisely how we would use the English word today—reliability, stability, and trust.

Often we may say to our students: "Don't forget to be loving and faithful." Daily we show our students how such a life of loving faithfulness looks. With consistency we must remind them of the techniques which achieve such a relationship: "Bind them around your neck, write them on the tablets of your heart."

> "Christian teachers share responsibility with parents in creating a value system which gives young people the opportunity to live rich and fruitful lives before God."

The metaphors remind us that these godly graces are both internal and external. Internally we can be loving and faithful because God writes that kind of behavior on our hearts through the Holy Spirit. Outwardly, we wear love and faithfulness like a beautiful necklace, adorning our appearance not through pride in the trinket, but in the loved One who gave it.

In 1873, William J. Lyons wrote a bit of verse which fits the metric pattern of Beethoven's "Ode to Joy":

O what glory, far exceeding, All that eye has yet perceived!
Holiest hearts, for ages pleading, Never that full joy conceived.
God has promised, Christ prepares it, There on high our welcome waits.
Ev'ry humble spirit shares it; Christ has passed the eternal gates.

Life eternal! Heav'n rejoices; Jesus lives, who once was dead!
Join we now the deathless voices; Child of God, lift up your head!
Patriarchs from distant ages, Saints all longing for their heav'n,
Prophets, psalmists, seers, and sages—All await the glory giv'n.

Life eternal! O what wonders Crowd on faith; what joy unknown,
When, amidst earth's closing thunders, Saints shall stand before the throne!
O to enter that bright portal, See that glowing firmament;
Know with Thee, O God Immortal, Jesus Christ whom Thou has sent!

Of course Lyons is talking about the Resurrection and the eternal hope in heaven. But those promises depend upon a loving and faithful God who serves as the model for how those characteristics must be developed in ourselves and our students.

DON'T FORGET TO TRUST THE LORD

Trust in the Lord with all your heart
    and lean not on your own understanding;
in all your ways acknowledge him,
    and he will make your paths straight.
(Proverbs 3:5–6)

"We are all walking commercials for God's grace."

In our passage we hardly find a group of unattached sayings such as appear later in the book of Proverbs. Instead the writer seems to build a logical progression, an argument for a wise and godly lifestyle. Even if the reader can expect long life and prosperity while enjoying a good reputation with God and people, he must totally depend on the Lord for everything. She must not assume that human understanding, however highly developed through education and experience, can achieve the elusive goal.

Within the last six months before writing this chapter, I've struggled with the agonizing death of a friend. For reasons known only to God, a young wife and mother of two children, actively involved in ministry and continuously reflecting Jesus Christ, was snatched to heaven. For months we watched her suffer and finally watched her die. At the memorial service, several testified of her stubborn trust in the Savior before the illness, during the illness, and right to the time of death. I found no human understanding to rely upon in such a painful situation. An experience like this makes us want to scream at the heavens and ask God if He really knows what He is doing.

When that scream, vocal or silent, reaches the gates of glory, the Father directs our hearts to a passage like this. No exceptions—in *all* your ways acknowledge Him and your path will be straight.

We are all walking commercials for God's grace; He has signed His name on our lives, often in the dark red ink of pain. Second Corinthians 12:9 has become a compass: "My grace is sufficient for you, for my power is made perfect in weakness." From the film *Shadowlands*, we hear C. S. Lewis saying, "God whispers to us in our pleasure; God speaks to us in our consciousness; God shouts to us in our pain. It is His megaphone to a deaf world."

TEACHER THOUGHT

"If I expect my students to acknowledge Him in all things, they must first of all see it demonstrated in my life." ~ Vicki, Ohio

DON'T FORGET TO FEAR THE LORD

Do not be wise in your own eyes;
fear the Lord and shun evil.
This will bring health to your body
and nourishment to your bones.
(Proverbs 3:7–8)

Every Christian school has its share of "wise guys," both male and female. Occasionally those types even show up in faculty ranks and, as we watch them, we remember that God does not want us to be wise in our own eyes.

Once again there is reward for following righteousness—health to the body and nourishment to the bones. It may help us to remember that in the context of Proverbs, the concept of healing may be spiritual and emotional though, as we noted earlier, those who walk circumspectly before God often receive better physical welfare as well.

Once again, however, a warning seems in order. Interpreting Scripture like this as a promise, either for ourselves or for our students, mishandles the text and leads to improper conclusions. After acknowledging the general statement of the proverb, we have to recognize that many very sick people fear the Lord and shun evil. *The presence or absence of health and wealth in our lives does not reflect accurately our relationship with God.* The proverb only affords a generalization.

Earlier I mentioned the death of a godly young woman. On January 20, 1994, George Burns celebrated his ninety-eighth birthday by entertaining a sell-out crowd at Caesar's Palace in Las Vegas where he is already booked for 1996. What a contrast! Does God really know what He is doing? Does the world really need George Burns and not need godly young mothers who reflect the Savior to their children and their communities? We have no human understanding for such a dilemma. We can only throw ourselves back on verse 5: "Trust in the Lord with all your heart and lean not on your own understanding."

DON'T FORGET TO GIVE

> *Honor the Lord with your wealth,*
> *with the firstfruits of all your crops;*
> *then your barns will be filled to overflowing,*
> *and your vats will brim over with new wine.*
> (Proverbs 3:9–10)

To speak of a wealthy Christian school teacher must be an oxymoron. Yet surely we understand that the concept of wealth is relative and in the days of Solomon as now, a farmer with a thousand acres or a farmer with ten both have some measure of "firstfruits." The proverb refers, of course, to Leviticus 23:10 and Numbers 18:12–13 where Old Testament law required Israelites to give to the priest the first parts of oil, wine and grain produced each year.

I daresay we who teach in Christian education do not address this subject often enough with our students. Perhaps our own giving patterns are sufficiently suspect that we do not feel competent or worthy to address the subject with others. In that case, we cheat God by not being generous with Him though our salaries may be low, and we cheat our students by not offering them this significant emphasis of God's Word.

I believe every Christian teacher ought to give regularly to the school where he or she teaches, and have followed this practice for over thirty-five years. If God has called me to a ministry, I feel an essential role in assisting that ministry financially, though my part may be small. Derrik Kidner offers a helpful balance to our passage.

> "Every Christian teacher ought to give regularly to the school where he or she teaches."

We tend to seize on verse 10, either critically or hopefully. But it must not steal the thunder of verse 9. To "know" God in our financial "ways" is to see that these honour Him; the honour will be compounded largely of homage (in giving Him the first and not a later share . . . of gratitude . . . and of trust, for such giving in the face of material pressures is a simple test of faith).[2]

DON'T FORGET THE VALUE OF DISCIPLINE

My son, do not despise the Lord's discipline
  and do not resent his rebuke,
because the Lord disciplines those he loves,
  as a father the son he delights in.
(Proverbs 3:11–12)

So life does not consist only of healthy joints and full wine vats; we also find struggle in our Christian walk. Obviously some of that may be brought about by our own irresponsible behavior. But here we learn that the Lord disciplines those He loves. We, His children, must neither despise nor resent that discipline. These verses, quoted in Hebrews 12:5–6, emphasize that suffering affirms our role in the family. Second only to parents as a leadership group, teachers must understand the purpose and practice of discipline. We all acclaim it, yet too often equate it only with corporal punishment.

But in the Hebrews passage the writer introduces teaching on both discipline and punishment as a "word of encouragement." The word "discipline," which appears in verse 5, occurs seven times in Hebrews 12 and emphasizes nurture and instruction. The word "punishment" in verse 6 appears only once and literally means "to beat." Doubtless corporal punishment has a role in both home and school, but it should never be confused with discipline. In fact, punishment is what we use when discipline breaks down.

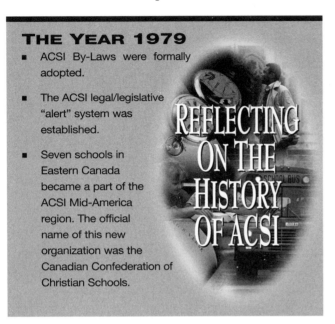

REFLECTING ON THE HISTORY OF ACSI

In the context of our Proverbs passage, discipline shows us another way God provides wisdom and keeps us on that straight path of verse 6. Let's be careful; not all life's struggles can be chalked up to God's discipline. Indeed, it would be quite inappropriate to identify the suffering of another as evidence of God's discipline in that life. This personal matter we must focus exclusively upon ourselves. Mature Christians understand that so much of what happens in their lives must be attributed strictly to the sovereignty of God and they assume God knows what He is doing and why He is doing it. Leroy Eims puts it this way,

It is the height of folly to think that God would bring anything to bear in our lives that was not for our very best. His correction never comes as that of a judge dispensing punishment; it comes as from a father who only wants to bring his children back to the safe path and a secure fellowship with himself. He corrects us because he loves us.[3]

> "Punishment is what we use when discipline breaks down."

"In all your ways acknowledge him"—more than a motto, our key verse suggests a lifestyle. If God allows us to influence hundreds of students over the years of our teaching ministry, it will be because we have fixed their eyes on Him by demonstrating loving faithfulness, trust, fear of the Lord, willingness to give and an acceptance of divine discipline. And what better place to achieve all of this than in a Christian school?

Let me close this chapter by borrowing another sentence or two from Willimon's article.

[Christian] schools are leading the way for a Christian rediscovery of a mission in education. If churches thought of the ideas that led to public education, we can think again creatively, providing visionary, revolutionary alternatives to the presumptuous and ineffective monopoly of public education… churches have much experience in exerting influence out of proportion to their numbers. And private Christian schools have a potentially very public witness by enacting new ideas that could become the salvation of a tottering public-education system.[4]

Willimon may very well be correct. Our focus should not center on whether or not the public system may crumble. We can heartily affirm the positive ministry God has given us with definite subservience to both Scripture and Savior. Our key phrase could very well be a standard logo for all Christian schools, perhaps even worn on uniforms and pinned to every teacher and administrator: "In all our ways we acknowledge Him."

ENDNOTES

1. William Willimon, "I Was Wrong about Christian Schools," *Christianity Today* (8 February 1993): 32.
2. Derrik Kidner, "Proverbs," *Tyndale Old Testament Commentary* (Downers Grove, Ill.: InterVarsity Press, 1964), 64.
3. Leroy Eims, *Wisdom from Above* (Wheaton, Ill.: Victor Books, 1978), 65.
4. Willimon, "Wrong about Christian Schools," 32.

CHAPTER THREE

A STUDENT WILL BE
LIKE HIS TEACHER

> into the ditch?
> 40 The disciple is not above
> his master: but every one that
> is perfect shall be as his master.
> 41 And why beholdest thou
> that is in thy brother's

Luke 6:37-49

I see it nearly every working day, sometimes more than once. Appropriately framed and nearly impossible to avoid, it stares back at me from the bulletin board in the faculty lounge. Other announcements come and go—scholarships available, schedules, special meetings—but this little plaque holds its space and says to everyone who walks into the room, "Everyone who is fully trained will be like his teacher."

Leaders have no choice about modeling. Parents, teachers, pastors may model well or they may model poorly, but model they will as children and young people watch. Interestingly our key text springs from an unlikely context. Luke devotes almost the entire sixth chapter to his version of the Sermon on the Mount, recorded at greater length in Matthew 5, 6 and 7. The context of our motto consists of the last three paragraphs of Luke 6, beginning with the warning against judging others, and ending with the parable of the house built on sand.

But, we must ask, in what ways will our students be like us? Will they dress like us? In some cases that may be true, but I can't think of a single Christian school teacher who would make that a goal. Will they think like us? To a great extent, the development of reasoning processes and plotting a life direction is very much a part of what we want to influence in our students. But Luke's context describes a behavior, notably what people do with other people. Indeed, these few paragraphs give us five different areas of life in which we can anticipate our students (as well as our own children) behaving like their mentors. We may expect that students will be:

LIKE US IN REACTION

Do not judge, and you will not be judged. Do not condemn, and you will not be condemned. Forgive, and you will be forgiven. Give, and it will be given to you. A good measure, pressed down, shaken together and running over, will be poured into your lap. For with the measure you use, it will be measured to you.
(Luke 6:37–38)

It seems axiomatic in professional football that the second player involved in a squabble draws the flag. Somehow officials fail to see the first punch or shove, but the reaction catches their attention and they assess the penalty. As much as we like to think about being proactive leaders, life creates surprises to which we must react, and those reactions often describe the kind of people we really are.

> "Life creates surprises to which we must react, and those reactions often describe the kind of people we really are."

Notice the command immediately preceding our passage: "Be merciful, just as your Father is merciful" (*v.* 36). What reactions form the opposite of mercy? Apparently judgment and condemnation. If we want to judge on earth, God will judge us. If we want to condemn others, we ourselves will be condemned. On the other hand, those who forgive receive forgiveness, and those who give receive generously from heaven.

Obviously, judging the work of others becomes a major responsibility of teachers. But here the context has nothing to do with grading or reporting student behavior. What happens when your students overhear another teacher speak unkindly to you? Your reaction (as well as his or her words) provides a lesson in living. As Proverbs 15:1 reminds us, "A gentle answer turns away wrath, but a harsh word stirs up anger."

Or think about your reaction to a critical remark by a student in class. Of course your superior wit and knowledge can chop him or her off at the knees; but again, your students will be like their teachers in reaction.

Luke speaks fluently of the magnificent mercy of God available to those who do not judge, do not condemn, but rather forgive and give. Lewis Smedes writes,

Forgiveness is not the alternative to revenge because it is soft and gentle;
it is a viable alternative because it is the only creative route to less unfairness.

Forgiveness has creative power to move us away from a past moment of pain, to unshackle us from our endless chain of reaction, and to create a new situation in which both the wrongdoer and the wronged can begin a new way.

Forgiveness offers a chance at reconciliation; it is an opportunity for a life together instead of death together. Forgiveness is a miracle of the will that moves away the heavy hindrance to fellowship, a miracle that will be fulfilled when the two estranged people come together in as fair a new relationship as is possible at that time and under those circumstances.[1]

LIKE US IN RESPONSIBILITY

He also told them this parable: "Can a blind man lead a blind man? Will they not both fall into a pit? A student is not above his teacher, but everyone who is fully trained will be like his teacher." (Luke 6:39–40)

Commentators struggle with the relationship of these two verses. Why does Jesus link them this way? Is the leading blind man one of the Pharisees and the second blind man his disciple? Does He intend to tell us that if we listen to and follow the wrong teachers we'll end up in a pit with them? Perhaps, but I rather favor emphasis on the responsibility of the mentor rather than the fate of the follower. In Jesus' day, disciples dedicated themselves to the teachings and values of their mentors, whether religious or secular Greek philosophers. Jesus' disciples had already chosen to learn from Him, and He reminds them they must be like Him. And their disciples, soon to follow, increased significantly the level of responsibility.

Once again, we and our instructional colleagues stand in the biblical spotlight. Like James 3, this passage shines directly on us. We must have sufficient insight to lead those over whom God has given us some authority, and must expect that—in significant ways—our students will be like us. As we work with present and future student leaders, we set precedents for responsibilities in

THE YEAR 1980

- Drs. Paul Kienel and James Braley visited eleven Christian schools in South Korea and, in so doing, spoke to thirty thousand students! Some of the largest Christian schools in the world are in South Korea.

- The ACSI teacher and administrator certification programs were launched.

- The first Christian school teacher convention sponsored by ACSI in Canada was held.

REFLECTING ON THE HISTORY OF ACSI

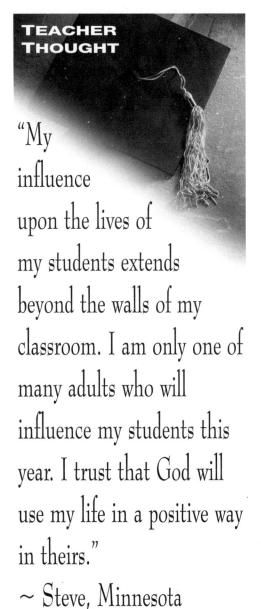

"My influence upon the lives of my students extends beyond the walls of my classroom. I am only one of many adults who will influence my students this year. I trust that God will use my life in a positive way in theirs."

~ Steve, Minnesota

relationships that the students will emulate. Although we may not think of it in such formal terms, students do mentor and disciple other students. We may ask ourselves, "Am I speaking the truth with love where correction shows itself necessary?" and "Am I ever abusive or excessively domineering with these students in a way that would cause them to think that type of behavior displays an appropriate leadership model?" Crawford writes,

> The school of God is for all believers and the teaching process goes on through the Christian life; however, we must understand this, in its context, as being special instruction for those who engage in the ministry of teaching. Being "like his teacher" is in relation to understanding, but we must also impress on our hearts that effective teaching will be manifest by a teacher who is morally like his Lord.[2]

LIKE US IN RELATIONSHIPS

Why do you look at the speck of sawdust in your brother's eye and pay no attention to the plank in your own eye? How can you say to your brother, "Brother, let me take the speck out of your eye," when you yourself fail to see the plank in your own eye? You hypocrite, first take the plank out of your eye, and then you will see clearly to remove the speck from your brother's eye. (Luke 6:41–42)

What a wonderful passage! So many familiar Biblical sayings gathered together by Luke in just a few verses, including this wonderful story of the speck and the plank. Jesus' admonition makes it clear that we cannot escape the responsibility of helping others with "specks in their eyes," but only after we have taken care of the larger sins in our own lives. All this takes us right back again to the issue of avoiding judgmental attitudes which we found in verse 37.

Perhaps we should always assume the *opposite* posture of the proud Pharisee who thanked God he wasn't a publican. He assumed the sins of others were greater than his own; we should consider our own sins greater than those of others. Such an attitude will drive us to the throne of mercy and will do wonders for our relationships with other people.

But let's not put all these warnings on the shoulders of the Pharisees alone. Jesus spoke to "a large crowd of His disciples" on this occasion, so the admonishment aims at believers as well. Our obedience must be voluntary and sincere, not demanded by a gracious God. *Sports Illustrated* magazine recorded that during the 1992 season, Chicago Cubs outfielder Andre Dawson paid a $1,000 fine for disputing a strike called by umpire Joe West. On the memo line of his check Dawson wrote, "Donation for the blind." Writing the check of self-evaluation is one thing, but we must also be willing to put our own guilt and blame on the memo line.

> "We should consider our own sins greater than those of others. Such an attitude will drive us to the throne of mercy and will do wonders for our relationships with other people."

LIKE US IN REPUTATION

No good tree bears bad fruit, nor does a bad tree bear good fruit. Each tree is recognized by its own fruit. People do not pick figs from thornbushes, or grapes from briers. The good man brings good things out of the good stored up in his heart, and the evil man brings evil things out of the evil stored up in his heart. For out of the overflow of his heart his mouth speaks. (Luke 6:43–45)

How often well-meaning Christians have maligned the intent of this passage. Frequently I have heard teachers and pastors renounce a judgmental attitude but affirm the right to be what they call "fruit inspectors," a posture which catapults them immediately back to the judge's bench. This passage has nothing to do with the inspector and everything to do with the production of fruit. To put it another way, Jesus claims that only good trees bear good fruit and only righteous hearts regularly produce truth. Here again we find an amazingly appropriate guideline for Christian teachers: "Out of the overflow of his heart his mouth speaks."

In the many sections of the New Testament which deal with qualifications for church officers, reputation repeatedly claims attention. In some cases we learn that the Christian

> "The concept of fruit... deals with the kind of life reflected by the words we use."

leader's reputation should even be affirmed by those outside the body of Christ. One could argue this passage in Luke says essentially the same thing. What is your reputation? Let's keep the parameters narrow and ask merely, what is your reputation among students in your school? Do those attending your classes affirm your fairness, Christlike spirit, gracious attitude and civility? Or have you cultivated and even take pride in a reputation as a harsh teacher, perhaps even a mean and grumpy one? The concept of fruit in this passage has virtually nothing to do with salvation; it deals with the kind of life reflected by the words we use.

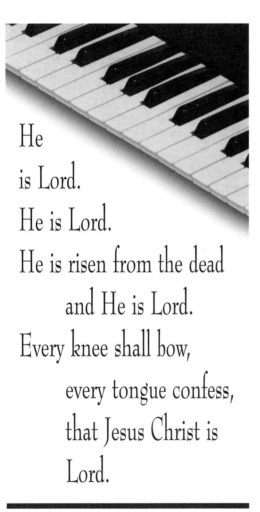

He
is Lord.
He is Lord.
He is risen from the dead
and He is Lord.
Every knee shall bow,
every tongue confess,
that Jesus Christ is
Lord.

LIKE US IN RELIABILITY

Why do you call me, "Lord, Lord," and do not do what I say? I will show you what he is like who comes to me and hears my words and puts them into practice. He is like a man building a house, who dug down deep and laid the foundation on rock. When a flood came, the torrent struck that house but could not shake it, because it was well built. But the one who hears my words and does not put them into practice is like a man who built a house on the ground without a foundation. The moment the torrent struck that house, it collapsed and its destruction was complete. (Luke 6:46–49)

The paragraph begins with a keynote question: "Why do you call me 'Lord, Lord,' and do not do what I say?" (*v.* 46). How convicting that question must have been for Pharisees and disciples alike when Jesus first spoke those words! Indeed, how convicting that question to the present hour, especially for those of us who have vowed to follow the Lord. The question is really quite simple— singing praise choruses and affirming a relationship with Jesus Christ do not provide the test of genuine Christianity. We find that test in the practice of obedience. The Lord refers to the matter of hearing His words and putting them into practice. In the lead question, the key word is *do*. What joy it gives us to sing genuinely, "He is Lord. He is Lord. He is risen from the dead and He is Lord. Every knee shall bow, every tongue confess, that Jesus Christ is Lord."

Every true Christian believes those words and most of us sing them with genuine conviction. The problem comes when we follow such singing with selective obedience, putting into practice those aspects of Scripture which suit us or provide minimal inconvenience, and willfully ignoring those which demand sacrifice and sometimes even pain. How easy to think of this parable as dealing only with a decision to trust Jesus as Savior and thereby gain eternal life. But the story seems broader than that. Builders do not merely select a site; they go about the process of building the house which, in this context, surely represents the lives of the hearers.

The House Built on Rock (*vv.* 47–48)

In this poignant portion of the so-called "Sermon on the Mount," the Lord talks about two ways, one broad which leads to destruction and one narrow which leads to life; two trees, one bearing bad fruit and the other good; and two houses built on different kinds of ground. Luke chooses the latter two contrasts to finish his record of the Lord's sermon and saves the narrow gate for later in his gospel.

One wonders what the audience thought of the emphasis on the rock. Certainly they understood the necessity of attaching a building's foundation to solid surface in a land where storms and flooding frequently occur.

But perhaps they saw in the Lord's words a deeper theology grounded on the Old Testament where the rock provides a strong symbol of the Lord Himself.

> "...perhaps they saw in the Lord's words a deeper theology grounded on the Old Testament where the rock provides a strong symbol of the Lord Himself."

> *Jeshurun grew fat and kicked; filled with food, he became heavy and sleek. He abandoned the God who made him and rejected the Rock his Savior.* (Deuteronomy 32:15)

> *You deserted the Rock, who fathered you; you forgot the God who gave you birth.* (Deuteronomy 32:18)

> *May the words of my mouth and the meditation of my heart be pleasing in your sight, O Lord, my Rock and my Redeemer.* (Psalm 19:14)

My salvation and my honor depend on God; he is my mighty rock, my refuge.
(Psalm 62:7)

The audience knew the Lord spoke not about issues of architecture and construction, but rather about the way people live. Their thoughts probably linked immediately to these and many other Old Testament references to the Lord as the Rock of Israel. So the one who hears the Lord's words and puts them into practice compares to a person building a house who dug down deep and laid the foundation on rock. The results? Jesus describes the house on the rock in no uncertain terms: "When a flood came, the torrent struck that house but could not shake it, because it was well built" (*v.* 48).

We dare not lose sight of the ultimate test of God's judgment, but let's not focus upon that. Trials, temptations, tragedies—all afford us present opportunity to measure the adequacy of our foundations and the excellence of our construction. Remember the third verse of that old children's chorus?

So build your life on the Lord Jesus Christ.
So build your life on the Lord Jesus Christ.
So build your life on the Lord Jesus Christ,
And the blessings will come down!

The House Built on Sand (*v.* 49)

It seems silly to picture someone deliberately building on a sandy floodplain, but that silliness forms the precise point of the parable. In actual fact, houses are built on floodplains all the time, and the owners act foolishly surprised when the rains come and wash away their holdings. People often do foolish things when it comes to Scripture and the Gospel as well. Whether we talk about housing construction or the development of one's spiritual life, we can honestly ask, "Why would someone do this?" Several answers suggest themselves.

Carelessness. Some home builders and life builders simply don't take sufficient care to find a suitable foundation.

Greed. Every major city could offer ample records of builders who constructed flimsy buildings because it seemed cheaper—at least in the short run.

Stupidity. Remember the Olympic athletes of 1992? How often in those interviews from Barcelona we heard about the years of self-denial and rigorous training, a surrender of the comforts of the present for the hope of the future. Those athletes showed wisdom in their choices to reach their life goals; in contrast, indulgence and soft living would reflect stupid choices.

Stubbornness. Every state, province, and country contains people who resist the conventional wisdom about building and say, "Don't tell me where to build my house."

Inconvenience. Finding a suitable place to build and constructing a strong foundation bring trouble and expense, something too many life builders do not want to bother about.

> "The issue is practice not profession; doing not hearing; solid orthopraxy not just sufficient orthodoxy."

Time. It takes time to build a good house and it takes time to build a good life. This parable is about more than just finding a place to build; it deals with the very construction itself.

What about the test results for foolish building projects? The Lord uses the words "collapse" and "complete destruction" which remind us of the sandy theology so typical of many modern religious movements. *The Expositor's Bible Commentary* puts it this way:

> A wise person represents those who put Jesus' words into practice; they too are building to withstand anything. Those who pretend to have faith, who have a merely intellectual commitment, or enjoy Jesus in small doses are foolish builders. When the storms of life come, their structures fool no one, above all not God.[3]

The issue is practice not profession; doing not hearing; solid orthopraxy not just sufficient orthodoxy. This issue of hearing and doing appears other places in Scripture (Luke 8:21; John 13:17) but never more poignantly than in James 1:22–25:

> *Do not merely listen to the word, and so deceive yourselves. Do what it says. Anyone who listens to the word but does not do what it says is like a man who looks at his face in a mirror and, after looking at himself, goes away and immediately forgets what he looks like. But the man who looks intently into the perfect law that gives freedom, and continues to do this, not forgetting what he has heard, but doing it—he will be blessed in what he does.*

At 5:04 P.M. on October 17, 1989, I was pushing two babies in a dual carriage on a sidewalk in Carmel, California. My legs began to tremble, and for just a second or two, I lost control. The great "World Series earthquake" had hit. For several days the world viewed television reports of destruction and chaos of the Bay Bridge, interstate highway connectors, and other places around the San Francisco Bay area. That's the kind of spiritual or moral destruction which comes to those whose lives have been built on sand rather than the Rock, Jesus Christ.

> "Like parents, we reproduce ourselves every day in the classroom, and that responsibility coupled with its parallel reward should drive us to our knees in both thanks and appeal."

Our key verse affords us both gratifying and terrifying possibilities. But the Scripture affirms the axiom that "everyone who is fully trained will be like his teacher," so we have enormous modeling responsibilities. Furthermore, we may not excuse the outcomes by suggesting that a student who does not measure up simply has not been "fully trained." Like parents, we reproduce ourselves every day in the classroom, and that responsibility coupled with its parallel reward should drive us to our knees in both thanks and appeal.

ENDNOTES

1. Lewis B. Smedes, *Forgive and Forget* (Carmel, New York: 1984), 131.
2. Norman Crawford, *What the Bible Teaches, Vol. 7* (Kilmarnock, Scotland: John Ritchie, LTD, 1989), 114.
3. Walter L. Liefeld, "Luke," *The Expositor' Bible Commentary*, ed. Frank E. Gaebelein (Grand Rapids: Zondervan, 1984), 194.

CHAPTER FOUR

1981

INCREASING IN THE KNOWLEDGE OF GOD

of the Lord unto all pleas
ou, being fruitful in every good
ith work, and increasing in the 202
ve knowledge of God;
11 Strengthened with all
according to his

Colossians 1:9-14

A t one time in the not-too-distant past, Christian schools were coming into existence at the rate of two a day. Indeed whole systems of Christian schools sprang up almost overnight. We would commonly read about the "Valley Christian School System" or "Christian Unified Schools of San Diego."

Major publications like *U.S. News & World Report* and the *New York Times*, as well as Christian publications, reported this phenomenon with some frequency. The Association of Christian Schools International conducts teacher and administrator conferences which attract well over forty thousand participants all across the country. *Christian School Comment* is now mailed to over one hundred thousand people monthly.

Without question, the 1970s and 1980s saw major growth in the Christian school movement. Whenever something explodes, however, one must be careful of the fallout. The very success of the Christian school movement brings with it dangers of pride and elitism; and the better the school (in terms of educational quality), the more likely it will commit these sins.

Perhaps even more common than pride and elitism, however, is a failure to understand the distinctive purpose of a Christian school. We work in the knowledge business, but what distinct role do we play? What is our market share, so to speak, in education both in North America and worldwide?

Christian schools extend home and church and therefore participate in the general purpose of making students more Christlike. Some Christian schools include evangelism as part of their overall objectives, while others focus on the development of students who already profess a relationship with Christ. Perhaps this overall *Biblical objective* shines most clearly in Colossians 1:28–29: "We proclaim him, admonishing and teaching everyone with all wisdom, so that we may present everyone perfect in Christ. To this end I labor, struggling with all his energy, which so powerfully works in me."

From the Biblical objective, we draw a more general *educational objective* which might sound something like this: to search for and communicate truth. The difference between Christian and secular education involves *defining* truth. To the secularist, truth is relative and natural, taught to basically good minds. To the Christian, truth is absolute and supernatural, taught to minds affected by original sin.

> "To the secularist, truth is relative and natural, taught to basically good minds. To the Christian, truth is absolute and supernatural, taught to minds affected by original sin."

As an educator, I would be the first to affirm that education has done much to raise the quality of life in America. But as a Christian educator, I qualify that statement by insisting that education cannot redeem anyone in and of itself. Over and over, history has proven that education cannot do everything. If education could redeem a society, the Greeks, the Romans, or the Germans had hundreds of years to demonstrate that feat. History testifies to the ruin of people and our social institutions unless the God of creation intervenes.

The passage before us now rests earlier in the chapter from which I cited two verses above. The first fourteen verses of Colossians form its introduction. Paul prepares to express his personal interest in that church, to warn believers there against pagan surroundings, and to refute false teaching threatening the congregation. Knowledge plays a major role in the book, but not false knowledge or knowledge for intellectual purposes only, a common problem today that I call intellectual idolatry. Rather he calls for a commitment to the spiritual knowledge found in Christ. Right from the beginning, he focuses his readers on a portrait of the Savior.

PRAYER FOR KNOWLEDGE

For this reason, since the day we heard about you, we have not stopped praying for you and asking God to fill you with the knowledge of his will through all spiritual wisdom and understanding. (Colossians 1:9)

In the first eight verses Paul has greeted the church and expressed a prayer of thanksgiving. The call for thanks echoes throughout this book like the chorus of a familiar hymn (Colossians 1:12; 2:7; 3:15, 17; 4:2). The lyrics are punctuated by wonderful words like faith, love, hope, truth, gospel, fruit, servant, and minister. Paul expresses delight that the Colossian church is healthy, that the Gospel has spread all over the Mediterranean world, and that God can effectively use a young man by the name of Epaphras in Colosse.

As I read verses like this, I think of your school and mine. What a delight it would be to get a letter from the ACSI regional director extolling the spiritual health on your campus, the impact of Christian schools around the world, and a special tribute to humble servant leadership exercised by administrators and teachers at your school. In this context, Paul prays for additional knowledge for the Colossians. Come to think of it, that might not be a bad addition to the letter we just received from the regional director.

How dare I write that we need more knowledge? Every teacher is overwhelmed by the information explosion in every possible field. We cannot keep up with the journals and books flooding our desks, and must often express embarrassment when professional colleagues ask whether we have seen the latest article by a leading expert in phonics, speech therapy or Christianity and modern literature.

But we know Paul does not speak of *that* kind of knowledge, as valuable and important as it is. He asks God to fill these believers "with the knowledge of His will" (*v.* 9). Not because they are weak and struggling; verses 3 through 8 indicate that these brothers and sisters were strong and growing. Our verse begins "for this reason" indicating that their very spiritual health

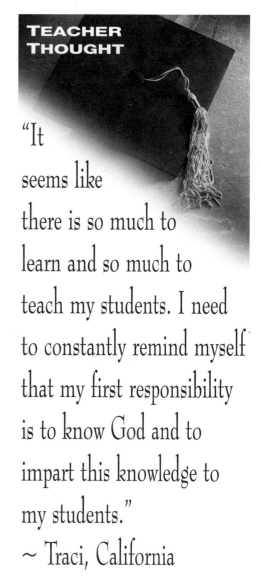

TEACHER THOUGHT

"It seems like there is so much to learn and so much to teach my students. I need to constantly remind myself that my first responsibility is to know God and to impart this knowledge to my students."
~ Traci, California

now enables them to move forward in spiritual knowledge. The first three words of verse 9 connect inseparably with the verses which precede it.

Sometimes we talk about the knowledge of God's will as referring to a specific decision—like changing jobs or buying a new house. In the context of this chapter, however, the broad plan of God for believers seems to be in focus. In-depth knowledge, therefore, refers to how we conduct our Christian lives in the vocation to which God has called us.

But there is another phrase of importance in our verse which qualifies "the knowledge of His will"—"through all spiritual wisdom and understanding." I doubt wisdom and understanding mean different things in this usage, but the way the verse unfolds certainly indicates that we arrive at the knowledge of God's will through spiritual discernment. I like the way A. T. Robertson put it decades ago.

Colossians 1:9
"Since the semester began, I have not stopped praying for you."
~ Teacher's Paraphrase

> The combination of wisdom and intelligence is what we all need and what Paul prays for on behalf of the Colossians. One may have intellectual attainments and a store of learning without being wise. There are learned fools as there are ignorant fools. In the knowledge of God's will both wisdom and insight are required.[1]

We can't rush on to the next verse without noticing Paul's prayer habits. The text literally reads, "We do not cease praying and begging for you." Certainly that seems appropriate terminology for an apostle and an early Christian congregation. But why not for a teacher in a Christian classroom in the 1990s? What if students arrived next Monday to find written on the corner of a chalkboard (just above that "do not erase" warning for the custodian) something like this: "Since the semester began, I have not stopped praying for you." Perhaps public display is unnecessary; a firm habit of the heart is not.

KNOWLEDGE

And we pray this in order that you may live a life worthy of the Lord and may please him in every way: bearing fruit in every good work, growing in the knowledge of God. (Colossians 1:10)

P aul does not keep us in suspense regarding the intent of his prayer. Knowledge of God's will, arrived at through spiritual discernment, should result in four specific behavior patterns. Surely it hardly stretches the boundaries of legitimate application to say Christian school teachers should:

Live a Life Worthy of the Lord

Creed and conduct walk hand in hand and spiritual enlightenment shows up in the real world (Philippians 1:27; Ephesians 4:1; 1 Thessalonians 2:12). The word "worthy" in this phrase is familiar to all educators who have dabbled in educational philosophy—*axiōs*, from which we get our word "axiology," a study of values. Paul stood constantly on guard lest anything he might do or say reflect negatively upon the Savior. Surely that kind of guideline provides light for our complicated paths as well. We consider our relationship with Jesus to be of worth, of value, and therefore we walk in that pattern.

THE YEAR 1981

- Paul and Annie Kienel attended the inauguration of President Reagan. Dr. Kienel was later appointed to President Reagan's key support group at a special luncheon in the State Dining Room at the White House.

- The ACSI school accreditation instrument became available for the first time.

- ACSI became a charter member of ECFA!

REFLECTING ON THE HISTORY OF ACSI

Please Him in Every Way

Interestingly the word for "please" suggests anticipating another's every wish. Husbands and wives living in proper Biblical relationship learn to do this almost as second-nature behavior. He likes his coffee a certain way so that's the way she fixes it. She needs to be told with some regularity that he loves her so he says it on every appropriate occasion.

Even children learn to anticipate what will bring a smile and a cheerful word from parents and teachers. For their own well-being and advancement, they seek to please those adult authority figures in every way. Sound idealistic? In today's rebellious society it sounds nearly impossible. But you and I know that Christian parenting and Christian schooling both target precisely that kind of behavior. Not from a false hypocrisy, but from the genuine desire to live that worthy life.

Bear Fruit in Every Good Work

The New English Bible renders the last phrase, "active goodness of every kind." The Colossians were already doing this, and Paul wants them to keep on doing it, so he uses the grammatical present tense. From the condemnation of John the Baptist in Matthew 3:8 to the Tree of Life in the last chapter of Revelation, the New Testament abounds with fruit-bearing allusions. Jesus frequently used this metaphor, invariably referring not to a Christian's ability to win others to Christ, but the outworking of faith in life. Again Robertson is helpful:

> "From Jonestown to Waco, we have been reminded in horror that when people do not believe the truth, the danger is not that they will believe nothing, but rather that they will believe anything."

We grow as we learn and bear fruit. Sometimes the loudest proclaimers of the truth are the poorest performers of it. Fruit bearing is more difficult than mere denunciation of error, but it is a more effective answer in the end. It is the best protection for those tempted by error. It is a sad situation if the orthodox have bad reputations, not to say bad characters.[2]

Fruit in the lives of teachers and parents may be the leading antidote to a society besieged with cultic error. This is not a grim specter on the horizon but a genuine omnipresent threat to the truth we teach. From Jonestown to Waco, we have been reminded in horror that when people do not believe the truth, the danger is not that they will believe nothing, but rather that they will believe anything.

Those of us who teach at all levels in Christian education must constantly warn our students of this danger. In our classrooms and counseling we must hammer home the truth of 1 John 4:3: "Every spirit that does not acknowledge Jesus is not from God. This is the spirit of the antichrist, which you have heard is coming and even now is already in the world."

Grow in the Knowledge of God

There's that "K" word again. It appears in some form no fewer than ten times in this short epistle. Like the admonition to bear fruit, the word "grow" takes the present tense, emphasizing lifestyle habits rather than some emotional event. One hardly needs to make some mystical explanation of a simple phrase like this. God has permitted us knowledge about Himself; it is our task to use what we have and gain more by bathing ourselves regularly in His Word.

In some ways, a good teacher performs like a skilled artist. Both create things of beauty through hours of toil and the application of training and dedication to the task. In addition to general teaching skills, formal training, and knowledge of specific subject matter in an academic discipline, Christian teachers need to know how to handle the Bible, the first and final textbook of the Christian school. We say to our students precisely what Paul said to Timothy almost two thousand years ago:

> But as for you, continue in what you have learned and have become convinced of, because you know those from whom you learned it, and how from infancy you have known the holy Scriptures, which are able to make you wise for salvation through faith in Christ Jesus. All Scripture is God-breathed and is useful for teaching, rebuking, correcting and training in righteousness, so that the man of God may be thoroughly equipped for every good work. (2 Timothy 3:14–17)

RESULT OF KNOWLEDGE

> Being strengthened with all power according to his glorious might so that you may have great endurance and patience, and joyfully giving thanks to the Father, who has qualified you to share in the inheritance of the saints in the kingdom of light. (Colossians 1:11–12)

We may certainly describe our society as a culture plagued by chaos and confusion. Christian teachers cannot solve all society's problems but we can face the issues and learn to think in a Christian way about our world. Then we can teach our students to develop a theology, a worldview, and a lifestyle that apply the historic Christian Gospel to contemporary culture. Rather than merely admitting that society languishes in chaos and confusion, we can at least ask what we can do about it.

"Rather than merely admitting that society languishes in chaos and confusion, we can at least ask what we can do about it."

Again we say that knowledge has a purpose and that purpose does not reside in the acquisition of knowledge itself. Four things mark the Christian teacher growing in spiritual knowledge:

Power for the Task

If we must do battle with cultic confusion and cultural chaos, we stand in desperate need of divine power. The word for "strengthen" here is the same root used in Philippians 4:13: "I can do everything through Him who gives me strength."

> "I have been called to Christian education and the power for my task is not limited to my strength or even my need, but rather God's abundant supply—'according to His glorious might.'"

I confess that sometimes when I enter my office at the beginning of the week and see what has been stacked on my desk already, I feel overwhelmed. Then the Spirit of God reminds me that I do not have a job, I have a vocation. I have been called to Christian education and the power for my task is not limited to my strength or even my need, but rather God's abundant supply—"according to His glorious might."

Endurance and Patience

Wow! Where are they selling this stuff? As much as I detest standing in line, if I could buy some additional endurance and patience at a reasonable rate, I might be willing to camp out overnight like a rabid fan trying to get Super Bowl tickets. "Endurance" suggests the opposite of cowardice and despondency rather than a willingness to wait for something. "Patience" is simply the opposite of retaliation or revenge. It describes the teacher who puts up with a lot of nonsense in the classroom, perhaps with the same child week in and week out, because she knows that surely God is working in his life and someday he may be a modern Epaphras.

One of my favorite teaching stories is told by Maurine Mugleston who lives in Salt Lake City and likes to go to hockey games. As reported in the *Reader's Digest*, she said,

> I was ring side when one of the players rammed into the boards. As he struggled to regain his balance, he gasped, "There must be an easier way to make a living." "I'll trade jobs," I retorted. "What do you do?" he queried. "I teach sixth grade." "Forget it," he said and was gone.

Where does all this endurance and patience come from? By growing in the knowledge of God and being strengthened with His power and glorious might.

Joyful Thanks

Notice Paul doesn't introduce joyful thanks until after we have demonstrated endurance and patience. Apparently we can exhibit patience with such gloom and bitterness that our lives do not really honor the Savior as we learned earlier in the passage. Paul wants us to understand we must do this "joyfully giving thanks to the Father." Leave it to Paul to annoy us with a good example. Remember that amazing duet with Silas in the Philippian prison? Forget the game plan; forget lesson plans. If you and I can function in our classrooms day by day with joyful endurance and patience, nothing could stop the work of the Holy Spirit in the lives of our students.

Qualification for Inheritance

Apparently people praised and prayed for by others have an obligation to thank the Father for placing them in that enviable position. Now we add gratitude to our growing list of Christian graces which already includes spiritual knowledge, godly strength, endurance, patience and joy. We know we have no right to heaven and have done nothing to earn the blessings God gives us on earth. God qualifies us by His grace not only for eternal salvation, but also to be His earthly mentors for children and young people (2 Corinthians 3).

> "God qualifies us by His grace not only for eternal salvation, but also to be His earthly mentors for children and young people."

CULMINATION OF KNOWLEDGE

For he has rescued us from the dominion of darkness and brought us into the kingdom of the Son he loves, in whom we have redemption, the forgiveness of sins. (Colossians 1:13–14)

What proof do we have that God has called us both to salvation and to Christian education? The last two verses of our passage seem to suggest three elements of our spiritual standing:

Rescue from the Dominion of Darkness

As you know, darkness in Scripture symbolizes ignorance and sin. We do not have to reach far to find darkness today. Just tune in MTV some evening and watch what your students have been viewing before they come to class. Or catch a few movies on cable television. Somehow those of us who have grown in spiritual knowledge to the point at which we have allowed the Savior to unwrap the grave clothes of Satan's control must teach impressionable children and young people how to do the same.

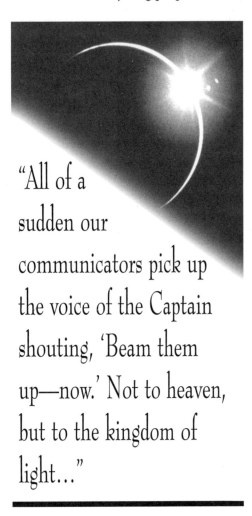

"All of a sudden our communicators pick up the voice of the Captain shouting, 'Beam them up—now.' Not to heaven, but to the kingdom of light..."

Reception into the Kingdom of His Son

Lightfoot translates this wonderful phrase, "He transported us thence and settled us as free colonists and citizens in the kingdom of His Son in the realms of light." It is as though we were wandering some scruffy little planet on an away team, bumping into strange creatures and dodging unknown diseases. All of a sudden our communicators pick up the voice of the Captain shouting, "Beam them up—now." Not to heaven, but to the kingdom of light operating in the fresh, crisp environment of a spiritual Enterprise, flying above the planets in the dominion of darkness in an effort to serve and save them.

Redemption—The Forgiveness of Sins

Should you ever need a simple definition of redemption, here it is in four simple words. First-century readers in Colosse would immediately recognize a word referring to the deliverance of slaves from bondage or prisoners of war from captivity. This spiritual emancipation proclamation is a present possession—we have it now. Redemption may mean a great deal more than forgiveness if we plumb its theological depths, but certainly without forgiveness of sins we have no redemption.

What a rich passage! So that is what Paul wanted for the Colossian congregation and what that mythical (but realistic) regional director prays for on your campus. Collectively we exercise the spiritual gift of teaching in accordance with the call of God. We pray for ourselves, for each other, for our schools, for our students and for the kind of spiritual growth and strength this passage glowingly describes.

ENDNOTES

1. A. T. Robertson, *Paul and the Intellectuals* (Nashville: Broadman, 1956), 34.
2. Robertson, *Paul*, 35-36.

CHAPTER FIVE

APT TO TEACH

> And the servant of the
> Lord must not strive; but be
> gentle unto all *men*, apt to
> teach, patient,
> 25 In meekness instructing
> those that oppose themselves;
> peradventure will give

2 Timothy 2:22-26

When Bettina Bunge retired from professional tennis, she had compiled a record of 0–17 against Martina Navratilova. Asked what she had learned from playing Navratilova, Bunge said, "How to shake hands."

This passage talks about shaking hands. It follows a portion of teaching on the issues of false doctrine and preparedness of the Lord's servants which includes the familiar fifteenth verse: "Do your best to present yourself to God as one approved, a workman who does not need to be ashamed and who correctly handles the word of truth." The previous paragraph ended with an emphasis on how those of us who serve the Lord are noble or ignoble vessels, either fit or unfit for the Master's use (see Chapter 1, "Prepared Unto Every Good Work).

Now Paul wants to talk about the practical dimensions of preparation and submission in offering us a contrast between kind people and quarrelsome people among the Lord's servants. I have adopted an outline reminiscent of a whole series of books by Warren Wiersbe in which each title begins with the imperative verb "be." Furthermore, rather than seeing "the Lord's servant" in our key verse (*v.* 24) as pastor, elder or deacon, we'll understand that phrase to apply to Christian school teachers.

Obviously in context Paul addressed a pastor, though there is no hint that these verses should be limited only to the historical recipient of the letter itself, Timothy. If the rules of hermeneutics seem hesitant to understand the passage more broadly, the rules of application actually require it. One could not possibly argue that God did not know Christian teachers would turn to passages like this in the 1990s for wisdom and direction in our attempts to be "the Lord's servants."

BE PURE

Flee the evil desires of youth, and pursue righteousness, faith, love and peace, along with those who call on the Lord out of a pure heart. (2 Timothy 2:22)

H ere we find another of those verses youth directors love to pull out at lock-ins and beside the weekend campfire. Since the Bible was essentially written by adults for adults, it's tough to find passages specifically related to teenagers. Verses like 2 Timothy 2:22 rank high on the list. But the word for "youth" in our passage appears only here in the New Testament. Timothy was already a pastor at Ephesus, probably in his mid-thirties at the time he received these words. A relative point, of course, since the aging apostle viewed a thirty-something pastor as young and very much subject to the lustful temptations around him. Both key verbs ("flee" and "pursue") take the present tense, suggesting the Lord's servants must be *constantly* fleeing and *constantly* pursuing (Romans 12:21).

> "We want our young people, both male and female, to see one another with healthy respect and holy affection."

The context of a Christian school cries out for a warning like this. It houses a group of attractive, intelligent adult instructors—some married, some not. In a freewheeling work atmosphere, any school provides opportunities to reverse these commands by pursuing evil desires and fleeing righteousness, faith, love and peace. How easy to think that sexual sin belongs to wealthy and visible television evangelists rather than to apply the warnings of this verse to ourselves.

As stated before, our students look to us for modeling behavior. We want our young people, both male and female, to see one another with healthy respect and holy affection.

In Christian teaching, we stand as a tiny pocket of resistance in a society already committed to moral destruction. Decay advances all around us. All week long we patiently drill righteousness and truth into student hearts and minds only to discover that Christian values have been battered and bruised all weekend by the latest audio and video releases.

One way to express that resistance to a degraded society lies in learning to treat faculty colleagues as well as students of either gender with dignity. Neither male bashing nor dumb blond jokes has a place in an institution where we stand committed to the proposition that all are created in the image of God.

Look at the balance of Scripture in these particular verses. The positive dimension outweighs the negative warning. The servant of the Lord pursues four valuable commodities of the Christian life: righteousness, faith, love and peace. The Bible calls for these, not with some isolated monasticism, but in community. We help each other pursue righteousness because we are all "those who call on the Lord out of a pure heart." The Christian school is one of many communities where you and your students find involvement. As we flee evil desires, we have the option, not of running to a sad and lonely vacuum, but of pursuing the kinds of virtues that build true communion among all believers.

BE COOL

Don't have anything to do with foolish and stupid arguments, because you know they produce quarrels. (2 Timothy 2:23).

The first six English words of this verse translate a single word. The New International Version has chosen a strong way to simply say "refuse moronic debates." Why? Because involvement in such foolishness inevitably leads to quarreling. Any ministry in which the servants of the Lord begin quarreling will be divisive and eventually useless.

Since education requires a constant process of mental activity, it holds great attraction for debate and, at times, foolish arguments. Faculty meetings or even board meetings can degenerate into precisely what this verse warns about. More common would be teacher/student squabbles in the classroom. Indeed, the word for "stupid" (which appears only here in the New Testament) describes an argument offered by uninstructed people using untrained and uneducated minds. None of this argues against sound debate of curriculum philosophy among faculty or a healthy and dynamic discussion in a senior Bible class. Disagreement or even conflict does not necessarily lead to quarreling; the pursuit of "foolish and stupid arguments," however, commonly yields unhealthy results. Those of us who make our living by talking must learn when to keep our mouths shut.

> "Those of us who make our living by talking must learn when to keep our mouths shut."

Let's not kid ourselves. Increasingly we will have to deal with children and young people who want to raise foolish and stupid arguments. According to a survey taken recently by *Leadership Journal*, only 16 percent of school-age children say they make moral judgments based on "what God or Scripture tells them is right." Forty-five percent say they make those judgments based on "their own personal experience." When foolish and stupid arguments arise, a Christian school teacher has to be cool. But cool does not mean wishy-washy.

> "The determination to live as a people pleaser can outweigh ethical and truthful answers. Such lack of moral courage provides no solution for staying away from quarrels."

Two men who lived in a small village got into a terrible dispute that they could not resolve. So they decided to talk to the town sage. The first man went to the sage's home and told his version of what happened. When he finished, the sage said, "You're absolutely right." The next night, the second man called on the sage, and told his side of the story. The sage responded, "You're absolutely right." Afterward, the sage's wife scolded her husband. "Those men told you two different stories and you told both they were absolutely right. That's impossible—they can't both be absolutely right." The sage turned to his wife and said, "You're absolutely right."[1]

This little parable illustrates a sad state of affairs: The determination to live as a people pleaser can outweigh ethical and truthful answers. Such lack of moral courage provides no solution for staying away from quarrels. Rather, I suggest discernment and careful thought before entering into discussion. Who among us does not know of people who simply love to argue, because they have developed skill at delivering verbal abuse or because they simply have foolish minds and too much time on their hands? With such folks we may make the decision to "be cool" and quickly disengage before finding ourselves caught in verbal traps and useless discussions.

BE KIND

And the Lord's servant must not quarrel; instead, he must be kind to everyone, able to teach, not resentful. (2 Timothy 2:24)

How often we think of our motto "apt to teach" as referring strictly to the spiritual gift of teaching. The concept of the teaching gift forms a significant block of New Testament text, but here the context argues *attitude* rather than *ability.* Even a person holding the gift of teaching, credentials to do so in the appropriate classroom, and experience as well, cannot share the Lord's truth with others when caught up in quarrelsome and divisive unkind behavior.

The first part of verse 24 echoes verse 23 but the behavior gets top billing, starting with kindness for everyone. The Lord's servant must be gentle with students and faculty peers as well. How we give nodding assent to a concept like this when thinking about a first-grade teacher patiently loving a group of children who adore her in return. Yet how distant this verse seems from the heat of a basketball game in which the coach of a Christian school team screams orders out to the court and spits sanctified obscenities to a player who turned the ball over and has just been summoned to the bench.

THE YEAR 1982

- Eastern Canada and Western Canada were established as independent regions.

- A building fund was approved as increased growth and the construction of a new headquarters facility were anticipated.

- A full-time business manager was added.

REFLECTING ON THE HISTORY OF ACSI

We cannot pick and choose our times to be kind and times to be quarrelsome. Nor do we choose people to whom we will behave in either of these ways. The command shoots as straight as a hired gun: "The Lord's servant must not quarrel; instead he must be kind to everyone." Christian school administrators have, in my opinion, an absolute responsibility to *enforce* this kind of behavior in every real-life situation from classroom to court, from study hall to soccer field.

You see, quarrelsome people are not "apt to teach" because their lives betray their lips. But what about those who take advantage of our kindness? Interestingly, once again the word translated "not resentful" appears only here in the New Testament and it describes the behavior of Christ. He endured the vile attacks of the Pharisees and the physical beatings of Pilate's henchmen only to pray, "Father, forgive them; they don't know what they are doing."

Please notice that our command requires a proactive stance. Avoiding the quarrelsome spirit of others must be *reactive*; advancing kindness demonstrates *proactive* behavior. As Frederick Faber once wrote, "Kind words are the music of the world. They have a power that seems to be beyond natural causes, as though they were some angel's song which had lost its way and came back to earth."[2]

We talk a great deal about modeling and mentoring, Filling our students' heads with knowledge, even Bible knowledge, will not produce kindness. That magical quality comes about in two ways: the Holy Spirit generates it from inside; you demonstrate it on the outside. That, my fellow teachers, provides an unbeatable combination.

BE GENTLE

Those who oppose him he must gently instruct, in the hope that God will grant them repentance leading them to a knowledge of the truth. (2 Timothy 2:25)

Obviously the Lord's servant must expect some to oppose the teaching of truth. Unfortunately we do not have the option given the disciples back in the Gospels of shaking off the dust of a city and moving on to the next when its inhabitants refused their message. Now, through the power of the Holy Spirit, we hang in there and keep teaching in meekness. Why? Because if we do so, God "may grant students repentance leading them to a knowledge of the truth." We don't have much problem believing God can do this; our complaint has to do with timing and that is precisely what Paul addresses in verse 26. But before we rush on to that verse, let's reflect on the contrast between Christian gentleness and the behavior of our society.

Perhaps someday a good psychiatrist can help me understand why I have always despised cruelty and brutality more than any other kind of wickedness on God's earth. Surely my childhood experience as the victim of bullies while growing up in the slums of a large eastern city accounts for part of my attitude. In today's world, few news stories move and anger me more than those about wife abuse, child abuse, slavery and torture. The hit movie *Schindler's List* penetrated my spirit and drove me to tears which lasted an hour after I left the theater. Apparently I was not alone; every person in that packed house rose silently and walked slowly toward the exit as though parading in a funeral.

Cruelty, brutality, violence and terrorism are fingerprints of the god of this world. He placed the boils on Job and sent the evil spirit to torment Saul. He caused the children of Israel to offer their infants in the burning arms of the god

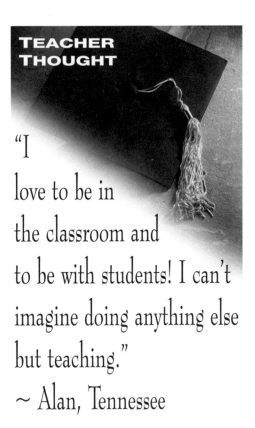

TEACHER THOUGHT

"I love to be in the classroom and to be with students! I can't imagine doing anything else but teaching."
~ Alan, Tennessee

Molech. And he watched with approval while they spat in the face of Jesus, drove nails through His hands, and slaughtered Him on a Roman cross.

The innate survival instinct in our surroundings activates our old natures and develops a callousness against cruelty. We want to retaliate with toughness, and better yet, to do unto others before they do unto us. Our verse denies us that option: "Those who oppose him he must gently instruct, in the hope that God will grant them repentance leading them to a knowledge of the truth."

BE PATIENT

And that they will come to their senses and escape from the trap of the devil, who has taken them captive to do his will. (2 Timothy 2:26)

The English phrase "they will come to their senses and escape" translates a single word in the Greek. People who reject the truth live in a theological and moral drunken stupor; sound teaching by kind people who refuse to argue is the antidote God uses to bring such people to Himself.

Who are these people? Those who have been caught in the devil's trap and taken captive to do his will. Paul hardly has in mind here some Satan-worshipping cult sacrificing animals on a cement slab ten miles out in the woods. These people worshipped in Timothy's Ephesian congregation. Any veteran Christian school teacher has encountered numerous students (and perhaps an occasional faculty colleague) who seem to be in a Satanic-induced drunken stupor when it comes to believing and acting upon the truth.

Some commentators interpret the latter part of our verse to mean that Satan has ensnared some to do his will and it is the task of Christian teachers to release them. Another view of the passage, however, suggests that the New International Version punctuation might be changed to indicate that those in the trap of the devil can be released to do God's will. I believe the grammar of the passage seems to favor the former suggestion but, in either case, the delivery system remains the same. Godly teachers who are pure, cool, kind, gentle and patient will be God's instruments in delivering

> "Godly teachers who are pure, cool, kind, gentle and patient will be God's instruments in delivering children, young people and adults from both resistance to truth and the trap of the devil."

children, young people and adults from both resistance to truth and the trap of the devil.

What a challenge we face in this final desperate decade of the century. How ill-equipped we often feel for the task of snatching people from Satan's trap through gentle teaching. Yet our passage could not be more plain. Men and women "apt to teach" must possess much more than credentials and experience; they must function in a climate of kindness and patience which makes possible the power of the Spirit in their lives, families and classrooms. May there be no lack of passionate intensity on the part of those of us God has called to the ministry of truth-teaching.

ENDNOTES

1. David Moore, "Laughter, the Best Medicine," *Reader's Digest*, February 1993, 58.
2. Frederick Faber, *Reader's Digest*, July 1986.

CHAPTER SIX

TO WHOM MUCH
IS GIVEN

> did commit things worthy
> stripes, shall be beaten with few
> 19. *stripes.* For unto whomsoever ca
> much is given, of him shall be 3
> much required: and to whom
> have committed much,

Luke 12:42-48

One short but complicated paragraph will be repeated dozens of times today throughout the United States. Those who use it don't want to say it. Those who hear it don't want to receive it. For some it's routine; for others, frightening. These are words you want to avoid. But be careful because sometime, somewhere, somebody might walk up to you and say:

You have the right to remain silent. Any statement you make may and probably will be used in evidence against you at your trial. You have the right to have a lawyer present to advise you either prior to any questioning or during any questioning. If you are unable to employ a lawyer, you have the right to have a lawyer appointed to counsel with you prior to or during any questioning. You have the right to terminate the interview at any time. (Version used in Dallas County, Texas)

This is, of course, the famous "Miranda" statement, which stems from the trial of Ernesto Miranda more than thirty years ago. On March 3, 1963, an eighteen-year-old woman employed by a Phoenix theater was kidnapped, driven into the desert and raped. Ten days later police arrested Ernesto Miranda and interrogators persuaded him to confess.

But that twenty-three-year-old indigent and the officers who arrested him found themselves caught in the vortex of history. For on June 13, 1966, the

Supreme Court upset the conviction and the decision, labeled "Miranda versus Arizona," became practice for every officer in America. You might remember the wording differently from television police shows, but Miranda warnings in some form are now the law of the land based on an interpretation of the Fifth Amendment.

The court decision didn't necessarily aid Ernesto Miranda himself. On February 24, 1967, a jury again found him guilty of rape and kidnapping (without the confession). He was sentenced to prison for a term of twenty to thirty years, and on December 12, 1972, paroled.

Perhaps more than any other words in America, the Miranda warning illustrates a society obsessed with rights. We have observed in the last twenty years a focus on civil rights, women's rights, children's rights, rights of the aging, rights of incarcerated prisoners and probably a dozen more types. Americans learn at a very young age to say to a playmate in a sandbox, "Hey, move over! You're violating my rights."

Who could forget the chilling paragraph Paul Kienel quoted in *Christian School Comment* early in 1994.

> Under the terms of the U.N. Convention on the Child, the United Nations grants power to participating governments to determine children's rights in isolation from parents, family and community. Parental rights and responsibilities in relation to their children are to be determined by the State and ultimately by the United Nations. The United Nations, as a deliberative body with multiple economic networks, international participants, and a variety of enforcement capabilities, would retain jurisdiction.[1]

As extreme as such rhetoric may be, we stand firmly within a rights-oriented society which hardly reflects the attitude the Bible calls forth from the servants of Jesus Christ. The focus of the Scripture centers on *responsibility* rather than rights. Christian teachers are "slaves," a metaphor regularly used to describe believers in the New Testament. And slaves have virtually no rights in relationship to their masters. Of course, our focus here rests neither on levels of pay nor volume of work but rather attitude toward duty.

In the twelfth chapter of Luke, Jesus teaches the crowds and His disciples about *witnessing, greed, anxiety,* and *readiness* for His return. Verses 35–48 contain two parables separated only by a question in which Peter asks: "Lord, are you telling this parable to us, or to everyone?" (*v.* 41). The second parable explains the first and sounds like this:

> The Lord answered, "Who then is the faithful and wise manager, whom the master puts in charge of his servants to give them their food allowance at the proper time? It will be good for that servant whom the master finds doing so when he returns. I tell you the truth, he will put him in charge of all his possessions. But suppose the servant says to himself, 'My master is taking a long time in coming,' and he then begins to beat the menservants and maidservants and to eat and drink and get drunk. The master of that servant will come on a day when he does not expect him and at an hour he is not aware of. He will cut him to pieces and assign him a place with the unbelievers.
>
> "That servant who knows his master's will and does not get ready or does not do what his master wants will be beaten with many blows. But the one who does not know and does things deserving punishment will be beaten with few blows. From everyone who has been given much, much will be demanded; and from the one who has been entrusted with much, much more will be asked."
> (Luke 12:42–48)

My treatment of this text promises no detailed exposition, but rather five simple observations as I see them relating to your life and mine.

CHRISTIAN SCHOOL TEACHERS ARE SERVANT LEADERS

We notice immediately in our text that the servant of our parable is a faithful and wise household manager in charge of other servants. The same word appears ten times in the New Testament, rendered variously as "steward," "chamberlain," "governor" and, in the *Modern Language Bible,* "custodian." This parable represents the first time the concept is applied to those who follow the Lord, but Paul picked it up thoroughly when noting that managers must be found faithful (1 Corinthians 4:2) and blameless (Titus 1:7).

The issue of leadership surfaces in the passage, not only in the noun, but also the verb. The master *appoints him* or *puts him in charge* of the other servants, a word Luke also uses in Acts 6 to describe the selection of the seven. Paul applies it in Titus 1:5 to speak of ordaining elders.

We are tempted here to think of administrators who seem to fit more closely with the Biblical concept of household manager or steward. But in reality, God has placed every Christian school teacher in charge of a class or classes of students, and many of the rest of us supervise peers as curriculum directors, chairpersons of committees, and in numerous other ways. We cannot dodge the requirement of leadership by narrowing its definition.

> "We cannot dodge the requirement of leadership by narrowing its definition."

The concept of servant leadership dominates the parable. One of the servants has become *head servant*, but his task calls for *feeding* the other servants, not *bossing* them. Earlier in this chapter, Luke introduced us to a master who serves when the first parable talks about the return from the wedding banquet. When he comes and finds ready servants "he will dress himself to serve, will have them recline at the table and will come and wait on them" (*v.* 37).

Not all Christian teachers hold exactly the same philosophy of education. But all must certainly agree that only servant leadership is truly Biblical. Servant leadership revolves around an attitude—the way we think about other servants and about ourselves in relationship to them. One church leadership expert talks about the difference between *shepherds* and *ranchers*—a valid distinction in ministerial types. Let's also make a distinction between *shepherds* and *wardens.*

I heard of a man who applied for a job as a prison warden. The personnel committee asked, "These are really tough guys in here. Do you think you can handle it?"

"No problem," the applicant replied. "If they don't behave, out they go." Too many of the Lord's teachers think like that.

CHRISTIAN SCHOOL TEACHERS MUST FEED AND SUPERVISE OTHER SERVANTS

The context obviously instructs first the apostles. Down through the ages it applies as well to those who, like them, agree to be the Lord's leaders. Please notice that slaves get no option. When Joseph rose from slave ranks to take charge of Potiphar's household, he had no chance to deny the appointment.

When the heavenly Master puts us in charge of other servants (students, faculty, staff), wherever the place and whatever the particulars, obedience is the only response. And our primary task is not to rule the other servants but to feed them and to do so in an orderly way ("at the proper time"). Servant leaders who have the responsibility for feeding other servants should not take themselves too seriously.

NFL fans remember John Brodie, at one time the starting quarterback for the San Francisco 49ers. One day in an interview he was asked by a reporter why he, such an important member of the 49ers team, had to hold the ball for point-after-touchdown kicks. Brodie replied, "Because if I didn't, it would fall over."

That response may or may not indicate self-effacing humility on Brodie's part, but it does depict the kind of tone the Scripture calls for on the part of God's managers. Like the Master Himself, the servant leader says to the other servants, "I am among you as one who serves."

THE YEAR 1983

- Dr. Francis Shaeffer spoke to 6,518 delegates at the ACSI teacher's convention in Anaheim, California.

- As a result of growth in Eastern Canada, a part-time regional director was added.

REFLECTING ON THE HISTORY OF ACSI

CHRISTIAN SCHOOL TEACHERS KNOW THE MASTER WILL RETURN

The Second Coming provides one of the dominant themes of this double-headed parable. When the Lord returns, the servant will be blessed if he's doing what he's supposed to do. Some Bibles headline this section "The Unfaithful Servant," and certainly that character comes in for his amount of attention in the latter part of our text. But the early verses focus on the faithful servant.

I don't know about you, but I've had my fill of superstar Christianity. Too often Christian magazines, radio and television give the impression that highly visible performance or size of congregation and school mark the plumb lines of God's blessing. But that view requires an anti-Biblical handling of the facts. Grandeur and ostentation display precisely what the Master does *not* want of us. He asks instead integrity, steadiness and dependability. Teaching and leadership compose a trust and those who have been given a trust must prove faithful.

I repeat for you some words which appeared in *Christianity Today* from the dynamic pen of Dr. Vernon Grounds, former president of Denver Seminary.

In our colleges and seminaries we infect students with the virus of worldly success. We communicate the message that success in God's service is to be an evangelist like Billy Graham or an author like Hal Lindsey or a pastor like Robert Schuller or a visionary like Bill Bright. Maybe we have been failing to communicate a clear-cut Biblical understanding of success. And, therefore, we fail to prepare our students for failure.

Do we really believe that worldly success is wood, hay and stubble? We need to remember how often the church will judge us the way the world does. Before anyone decides on a full-time ministry, for example, he must realize that God may be calling him or her to a ministry of tedious mediocrity… Each of us must have the faith to keep serving even if unappreciated, unsung, and unapplauded—in short, we need a faith to face failure.[2]

Grounds' point, of course, shows that failure in the eyes of the world may very well be success in the eyes of God if the servant has focused on faithfulness rather than flashiness. When the Lord comes, you may be serving in a tiny school somewhere south of Cleveland, struggling to keep a student body of one hundred true to God's Word. Nobody of "importance" in the country may know where you are; but don't worry, the Lord will find you.

Perhaps you'll teach in Pennsylvania where God must search through towns and villages with fascinating names to call His servants home.

On one side of Desire, Pennsylvania, is Paradise. On the other side is Panic. The villages are clustered above Punxsutawney, which in Delaware Indian refers to the gnats that plague the area; in other words, "Bug Town." Those Pennsylvania pioneers sure had a sense of humor. Scattered among the hills and valleys of central and western Pennsylvania are an amazing number of places you can be grateful you don't have to give as your return address—and some you can be proud of, too. Within a few hours, you can flit from Bird in Hand to Pigeon by way of Eagle, Larke and Oriole. Lemon and Nectarine, Orange Plum and Cherry Tree are all in the same neck of the woods. There's a Youngstown and Eldersville, Abbot and Costello, Tally Ho, Forty Fort, Five Points and three towns each named Seven Stars.[3]

So be not afraid to go wherever He sends you and take whatever position He gives, regardless of how "invisible" it may seem. When the Master returns, He will find us all no matter where we serve.

I'm fascinated that the reward for faithful work is more work. I dare say that principle hasn't changed in two thousand years of church history. Look again at verse 44: "I tell you the truth, he will put him in charge of all his possessions." At first that promotion looks like a reward and, of course, in a real sense, it is. But it also brings greater responsibility, the responsibility of privilege. Stuart Briscoe writes of this passage.

> I am convinced that a true sense of privilege is one of the greatest possible motivating factors, [but] the value of being in such a relationship is determined by a consideration of the owner and the master and his attitude to his servants. . . . if he is known to be the sort of person who will sit servants down at the table and make a meal for them occasionally it would be reasonable to assume that potential servants would be standing in line waiting for the old servants to die off and the stupid ones to be fired.

As for Joseph, small tasks well done lead to greater tasks and harder work. Good teaching leads to more challenging classes, committees and supervision and, at the same time, a fitting reward and a greater responsibility. A Christian leader, by definition, goes beyond the call of duty without constantly calling attention to safe limitations and to his or her rights.

Where do you serve? In a comfortable middle-class school of one thousand in Orange County? If that's where God called you, that's the only place to be. But please keep in mind that the United States is the largest Jewish nation in the world. For years it has also been the largest Irish nation. It is the second largest Black nation in the world since only Nigeria, of all fifty-three countries of Africa, has more people of African descent than the United States.

Currently only Mexico and Spain have more Spanish people than the United States. More people use sign language in the United States than live in all the countries of Central America. More Polish people reside in Chicago than the entire populations of either San Francisco or Seattle. Remember when we used to talk about "going to the mission field"? It has come to us.

But let us not forget about the new horizons of ACSI ministry overseas. One need only hear Phil Renicks speak for fifteen minutes to understand that the command "lift up your eyes and look on the fields" no longer applies only to disciples and missionaries. Christian school teachers face global opportunities never before available.

A world-class city contains at least a million people. By the year 2000, this globe will boast nearly five hundred world-class cities. In Mexico City, a Seattle-sized city of babies is born every year; a Milwaukee-sized city of immigrants move in every year. The economy of Mexico City requires a million new jobs every year. The median age there stands at 14.2. The oldest city in our hemisphere is also the youngest! No city in the third world has a median age of over twenty, and 87 percent of babies born in the world have parents of color.

You say you need space to grow and develop? Have you considered Africa? All of the United States, all of China, all of Argentina, all of India, and all of Europe fit on the map of Africa which contains 11,706,166 square miles. We face a country and a world in desperate need.

CHRISTIAN SCHOOL TEACHERS MUST UNDERSTAND THE PUNISHMENT FOR MISLEADERSHIP IS SEVERE

It is my intent to focus only on the faithful servant so I treat the latter part of the parable rather quickly. Some distinguished commentators suggest it is metaphoric, others indicate we have here an indication of degrees of both punishment and reward at the appropriate time of judgment. One thing seems clear—God expects the servant to know his master's will and to do it.

How did Peter understand all this after his question in verse 41? Just a guess, of course, but I suspect the last half of verse 48 rang in his ears much as it has in mine day after day for decades of ministry: "From everyone who has been given much, much will be demanded; and from the one who has been entrusted with much, much more will be asked." The central idea of the parable demands that serving the Lord is a matter of responsibility not rights.

> "Serving the Lord is a matter of responsibility not rights."

This closing principle forms a veritable New Testament proverb which warns us that God will hold you and me—people who have had unparalleled and in some ways unprecedented privileges—responsible for greater performance in ministry.

Passages like this seem to be divine attention-getters. After being hit by lightning on the golf course, Lee Trevino was asked what he had learned from the experience. "When God wants to play through," he answered, "you'd better let Him!"[4]

Perhaps a fitting close to this chapter might offer a paraphrase of that famous Miranda warning.

Christian teachers have the right to unquestioned obedience. Any statement we make may and probably will be used in evidence either for or against the cause of Jesus Christ. We have the right to have the Holy Spirit present to advise us in our classrooms. If we choose not to carry out ministry on the Master's terms, we have the right to leave Christian school teaching and work someplace else.

ENDNOTES

1. Paul A. Kienel, "The Children's Rights Movement: Something to Pray About," *Christian School Comment* 25, no. 67 (1994).
2. Vernon Grounds, "The Faith to Face Failure," *Christianity Today*, 9 December 1977, 11–13.
3. Timothy Middleton, "From Desire to Panic," *Reader's Digest*, July 1993, 99.
4. "Star Struck," *Reader's Digest*, June 1992, 156.

CHAPTER SEVEN

FOR YE SERVE
THE LORD CHRIST

> 24 Knowing that of the L
> the ye shall receive the reward of
> the the inheritance: for ye serve
> the Lord Christ.
> 25 But he that doeth wrong
> receive for the wron

Colossians 3:22-4:1

During the summer after my sophomore year in college I had the opportunity to travel to Europe with a gospel team, a life-changing experience which reoriented me into ministry. However, gospel team travel for an entire summer provided no opportunity to earn money for the following fall so I found myself working throughout my junior year at the RCA television tube manufacturing plant in nearby Marion, Indiana. My shift dragged from 11:00 P.M. to 7:00 A.M. and, during that time, I continuously carried thirty-five-pound television tubes from conveyor belts to a rack and back again. That dreadfully boring and fatiguing work drove me many a morning to remind myself, "I'm doing this now so I don't have to do it the rest of my life."

The job got me through the year and I learned a great deal about perseverance, but the motivation fell far short of the Biblical pattern God has set for His people. We find it in Colossians 3 where the apostle writes, "Whatever you do, work at it with all your heart, as working for the Lord, and not for men" (*v.* 23). Amazingly, this verse appears in the midst of a passage written to slaves, of which more than 60 million roamed the Roman Empire during the first century. More than half the people on the streets of its cities were slaves—and they included most of the doctors and teachers in the realm.

It seems fitting to find motivation for Christian school teaching in a slave passage. To be sure, we have come a long way in salaries and working conditions for teachers. However, the priorities of North American society have not changed, as I have observed before. As I write these words, *Newsweek* magazine has just announced the salaries of network news anchors— Tom Brokaw at $2 million, Connie Chung at $2 million plus, Dan Rather at $3 million plus, Peter Jennings at $7 million, Barbara Walters at $10 million. Diane Sawyer's recently negotiated ABC contract, reportedly running somewhere between $5 and $7 million, prompted the article in which *Newsweek* concludes, "At the risk of irking lesser stars and draining resources, the networks will continue the care and feeding of its brand names, just like soap and toothpaste. The question remains whether these brand names perform as journalists—or products."[1]

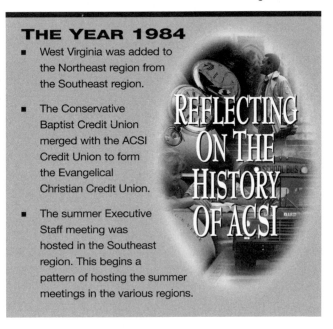

THE YEAR 1984

- West Virginia was added to the Northeast region from the Southeast region.

- The Conservative Baptist Credit Union merged with the ACSI Credit Union to form the Evangelical Christian Credit Union.

- The summer Executive Staff meeting was hosted in the Southeast region. This begins a pattern of hosting the summer meetings in the various regions.

Certainly I do not wish to imply that any of these superstars or their colleagues are motivated by salary rather than the pure love of news. But one thing seems brilliantly clear: motivation for Christian school teachers had better be love for teaching since the salary schedule will not likely catch up with the importance of the profession anytime in the near future.

This chapter describes motivation. In it I offer three perspectives of service or, if you will, three different work ethics. These attitudes apply both to repetitious work on automotive assembly lines in Detroit or to volunteer Sunday school teachers in a junior high class. Most importantly, they describe the way Christians think about the work they do and how those attitudes line up with the Biblical motivation described in our passage.

I SERVE MYSELF
The Buffet Ethic

Let's call this the "buffet ethic." Buffet meals suit our North American independent mentality. Never mind the waitress and all that family-style formality, we'll just go around the table and take what we want, serving ourselves. That's fine for culinary activities, but as a general lifestyle, such an attitude only depicts the materialistic society.

Unfortunately we often find it in ministry roles. Acts 8 tells of Simon Magus and Acts 13 of Elymas the sorcerer, deeply religious men, even claiming association with the God of the Old Testament. In both cases, however, they served themselves. Their fates (as identified by Peter and Paul respectively) jump at us from the pages of Holy Scripture.

> *When Simon saw that the Spirit was given at the laying on of the apostles' hands, he offered them money and said, "Give me also this ability so that everyone on whom I lay my hands may receive the Holy Spirit."*
> *Peter answered: "May your money perish with you, because you thought you could buy the gift of God with money! (Acts 8:18–20)*

> *Then Saul, who was also called Paul, filled with the Holy Spirit, looked straight at Elymas and said, "You are a child of the devil and an enemy of everything that is right! You are full of all kinds of deceit and trickery. Will you never stop perverting the right ways of the Lord? Now the hand of the Lord is against you. You are going to be blind, and for a time you will be unable to see the light of the sun." (Acts 13:9–11)*

Elymas called himself Bar-Jesus (son of Jesus), but Paul identified his true nature as a son of the devil. So even today Christians have a tendency to absorb the surrounding culture, to be sucked into the selfishness and egoism of late twentieth century North American society.

Too often we hear this attitude from those who know better. Teachers and administrators talk about size, personal prestige and lately even political clout, as though these somehow measure spiritual success. Of course they do not. They reflect the very secular humanism Christian school people claim to be fighting.

The Christian school movement has stood firmly against secular humanism, and properly so. But let's keep in mind the true enemy. There are secular humanists, religious humanists, and Christian humanists. Of the three categories only inhabitants of the first can properly be called atheistic, evolutionist naturalists. Religious humanists like Ghandi and Christian humanists like the brilliant Erasmus of Rotterdam or the twentieth-century apologist C. S. Lewis can get hit with fragments of our attack grenade if we are not careful where we throw it.

The ultimate issue is not, in my opinion, moral or political as many have claimed, but rather theological—the ultimate confrontation between those who support God's revelation and those who deny it. I raise this issue because segments of our movement seem in danger of being politicized. We all lose when someone takes Christian schools out of the hands of educators, philosophers and theologians and puts them into the hands of accountants, attorneys and politicians. I decry that. I oppose it. I warn of its present and impending dangers.

The tragic irony of the whole debate is that those who cry the loudest against humanism seem to fight hardest to take various levels of government into their own hands. They strive to gain by acts of political power what God has apparently forgotten or has not had time to do for His people.

At best such behavior demonstrates this self-serving buffet ethic. At worst it ignores and belittles the Scripture which warns, "The weapons we fight with are not the weapons of the world. On the contrary, they have divine power to demolish strongholds. We demolish arguments and every pretension that sets itself up against the knowledge of God, and we take captive every thought to make it obedient to Christ" (2 Corinthians 10:4–5). Taking thoughts captive to Christ in our classrooms forms the task of Christian teaching. Those who give their lives to such a goal have little time to threaten secular educators or state governments by their voting block influence.

> "Taking thoughts captive to Christ in our classrooms forms the task of Christian teaching."

The buffet ethic also corrupts the purity of our own service. The old nature stands at the center requiring that all else revolve around it. Humility and meekness, so often demanded in the Scriptures, absent themselves from self-serving mentality. I recall again the story circulated on national news services after eight candidates met for a debate at Dartmouth College early in 1984. As the audience filed from the debate hall, newswriters asked one young student what she thought of the debate and the candidates. She replied, "None of them seem to have any humility." Her evaluation provides a commentary on the whole attitude of our society and a political system in which self-serving and self-selling hold constant control.

Such an attitude stands in contrast with the words in the earlier part of our focus as Paul reminds the Colossian Christians,

> *Since, then, you have been raised with Christ, set your hearts on things above, where Christ is seated at the right hand of God. Set your minds on things above, not on earthly things. For you died, and your life is now hidden with Christ in God. When Christ, who is your life, appears, then you also will appear with him in glory.* (Colossians 3:1–4)

As Christian school teachers we face a greater responsibility than the immediate dangers of self-serving. I refer, of course, to the impact such behavior will have on our students. Self-serving teachers will produce self-serving students. Self-serving schools will create self-serving graduates. We must always keep the Biblical motive before us and before those over whom God has given us influence.

I SERVE THE ORGANIZATION
The Boss Ethic

Slaves, obey your earthly masters in everything; and do it, not only when their eye is on you and to win their favor, but with sincerity of heart and reverence for the Lord. (Colossians 3:22)

"Self-serving teachers will produce self-serving students. Self-serving schools will create self-serving graduates. We must always keep the Biblical motive before us and before those over whom God has given us influence."

Clear Mandate

Perhaps we can call this the "boss ethic," a common attitude for Christians and non-Christians alike with respect to their work. Indeed, Paul commends it in verse 22. This reflects the answer of moral religion and it represents dramatic improvement from the first option. If Jesus were speaking today, He probably would have referred to employees, not slaves. This provides a clear mandate: sacrificial and sincere service for a boss, an organization, a school, a church, a mission board—a Biblical response to earthly responsibility.

At one point in the history of Europe, King Wilhelm II of Prussia faced big trouble. There was no money left in the imperial treasury for wars and rebuilding. The king asked the women of the land to bring their gold and silver jewelry to be melted down. In return, they received a decoration of iron as a symbol. It was stamped, "I gave gold for iron, 1813." Surprisingly, women prized these symbols more than their jewelry for the decoration offered proof of sacrifice for their king. Jewelry actually became unfashionable and the Order of the Iron Cross was born.

Crucial Motive

The boss ethic also offers a crucial motive and the text speaks clearly on this point as well. The Christian teacher works hard not just while the boss watches,

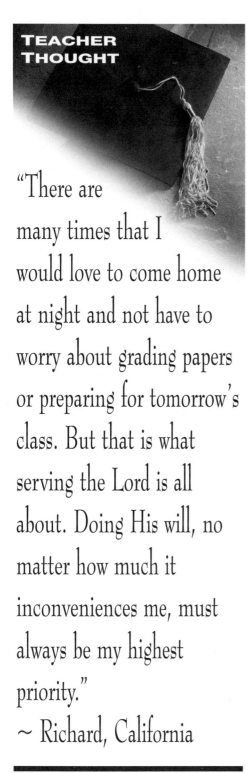

"There are many times that I would love to come home at night and not have to worry about grading papers or preparing for tomorrow's class. But that is what serving the Lord is all about. Doing His will, no matter how much it inconveniences me, must always be my highest priority."

~ Richard, California

and not just for recognition. Today, managment takes security measures in stores and businesses to protect against employee theft as well as customer theft. What kinds of things constitute theft in our environment? Simple things qualify, such as pilfering office supplies or using the copier for personal reasons without reimbursing the organization. But the problem may go much deeper. How do we use our time? Do we give careful attention to lesson plans and classroom activities so we don't waste the students' class hours? Do we grab those special "teachable moments" when they come, or carelessly let them fly from our grasp? According to the New Testament, Christians living righteously serve the organization with integrity.

Commanded Model

A third lesson in this passage provides a commanded model for bosses. Paul actually addresses them in the first verse of the next chapter: "Masters, provide your slaves what is right and fair, because you know that you also have a Master in heaven" (Colossians 4:1). So in our interpretative understanding of Colossians 3:22–4:1, slaves become teachers and masters, administrators. Of course, this text addresses supervisors of every kind—managers, foremen, pastors, principals, mission executives—all Christians share a common responsibility to model the behavior of integrity and honesty. Then service for the organization becomes a spiritual duty and even a daily joy.

We Christian teachers must constantly remember that our mission does not point to ourselves. Remember the Pharisees? Because of their station in life, they found it easy to draw attention to themselves. They liked their seats in the synagogues—up front—facing the congregation where their attendance and rapt attention to synagogue happenings could be seen and noted by all. Jesus said to them, "Woe to you Pharisees, because you love the most important seats in the synagogues and greetings in the marketplaces" (Luke 11:43).

Apparently, having been seen in the synagogue, the Pharisees would also be recognized on the street and given elaborate greetings which marked them as people to whom others show deference. Does any of this sound familiar in the contemporary church? How about in the Christian school movement? Renowned Christian leaders intimidate us average people simply by shaking hands. Why? Because our society segments "important" and "nonimportant" people and everyone had better know his or her place—rather like the British monarchy.

> "Christian teachers who want to be Biblical in their classrooms will reflect the homage of their students to the Christ who deserves it, and reflect the grace of that Christ to the students who desperately need it."

Christian teachers must always remember that they direct students' attention to Christ, not to themselves. We who teach children find it especially easy to allow a focus on our own persons. But the greatest commodity of a Christian school is not its teachers, its curriculum nor its students but the truth it handles day by day (see Chapter 15, "Teaching in All Wisdom"). Unlike the Pharisees, Christian teachers who want to be Biblical in their classrooms will reflect the homage of their students to the Christ who deserves it, and reflect the grace of that Christ to the students who desperately need it.

I SERVE THE LORD
The Biblical Ethic

Whatever you do, work at it with all your heart, as working for the Lord, not for men, since you know that you will receive an inheritance from the Lord as a reward. It is the Lord Christ you are serving. Anyone who does wrong will be repaid for his wrong, and there is no favoritism. (Colossians 3:23–25)

Rising far above the buffet ethic and the boss ethic is the Biblical ethic, the answer of committed Christians. The clear imperative of the passage implores believers to "work at it with all your heart." Only here in the New

Testament do we find the phrase "working for the Lord." And the context offers a distinctively Biblical work ethic. How can you and I actually make this work in the classroom and office? It seems to me at least three things are required.

1.   Christian school teachers and administrators must be assured that God has called them to this important work. Does God really want me in a science classroom rather than a laboratory? Am I really to be a computer teacher rather than a pastor? Has God called me to teach third grade in this Christian school? Am I following through in God's will for my life?

2.   Christian school teachers and administrators must be aware they are meeting needs. Those in any profession find it difficult to sustain the drudgery and monotony of some jobs over long periods unless they have some motivation other than just earning the paycheck. Industrial psychologists tell us there must be self-actualization, and the best kind comes with the knowledge that we're meeting the needs of other people.

Few occupations or even ministries fit this criterion better than Christian school teaching. Most sincere teachers are members of the helping professions, but those who handle absolute truth and apply it to all aspects of the curriculum meet needs even as yet unknown to their students.

3.   Christian school teachers and administrators want to be assured of God's blessing. If God can use me as a witness in the classroom, to share the Gospel with unsaved students, to be an encouragement to my faculty peers, or in some other significant way, then I can perceive of work as service for Christ.

How has God blessed your teaching? What evidence have you seen in the last year that the Holy Spirit has used the gifts He has given you to develop and disciple students in your school?

As human beings, we need encouragement to be encouragers. The kind of people who choose and stay in teaching as a vocation respond positively to evidence that they are channels of God's blessing. Christian teachers should enable students to achieve their highest potential—academically, physically, socially and spiritually. A Christian school should offer the encouragement, environment and equipment to make that kind of enabling possible. When we serve the Lord Christ, duty is no longer a negative concept. In our classrooms, control and order make possible learning and the disciplined life.

I have alluded several times to Colossians 4:1. Every boss has a boss and the biggest boss serves the Biggest Boss. There is an old line in the legal profession which, loosely stated, sounds like this: "Any lawyer who represents himself has a fool for a client." In the writing profession with which I am more familiar, we commonly say, "Every editor needs an editor." Those of us who hold responsibility over others of the Lord's servants bear greater accountability to Him.

This dynamic chapter in Colossians displays the work ethic immediately following a strategic family section. The early verses of the chapter deal with the Christian's own spiritual life, followed by the family section in verses 18–21. When these two dimensions of life come to order, we can properly turn our attention to serving Christ on the job. Success in the classroom must be interpreted in light of these bigger priorities. We doubt that anyone living in this fallen world has priorities in perfect order, but God finds unacceptable any service that perverts His priorities of personal spiritual life and solid family · functions.

Elizabeth Elliot tells a marvelous story, a fable in which the disciples were once asked by the Lord to carry stones throughout the day. Each chose the smallest stone he could find and, at evening, the Lord turned their stones into bread. With hungry stomachs they went to bed wishing they had chosen larger stones.

> "Those who really understand the motivational principles of the New Testament work to serve the Lord."

The next day He gave the same command. Imagine how the disciples scurried around selecting the largest rocks they could carry. As they made camp for the night Peter asked, "Lord, what will we do with our stones?"—expecting to feast on fresh bread.

"Oh," said Jesus, "just roll them into the river there." The complaining sounded like the Israelites of old and only quelled when the Lord asked, "For whom did you carry your stones today?"

Some Christian teachers may serve themselves; others may serve the school; but those who really understand the motivational principles of the New Testament work to serve the Lord.

ENDNOTES

1. Larry Reibstein, "A Star is Rehired, Fabulously," *Newsweek*, 28 February 1994, 58.

CHAPTER EIGHT

THE SOWER SOWETH THE WORD

ow then will ye know
ables?
or 14 ¶ The sower soweth the
word.
15 And these are they by the
side, where the word is
when they

Mark 4:1-14

One of my colleagues related this story: "My teenage son still talks about his first grade teacher who patiently and gently helped him through a difficult year of his life, faithfully presenting Bible truths skillfully woven among the other lessons. Always a difficult, hard-to-handle child, I often wondered if any of us were reaching him. Now he reads his Bible faithfully, takes his friends to church, and has made an apparently unbending commitment to living a life of personal morality. That teacher had a major effect on his faith and stability today, but I doubt she realized it at the time."

This faithful Christian school teacher sowed seeds; others reap untold fruitfulness because of her work. As a teacher, she nurtured her students while communicating truth. The passage of Scripture before us in this chapter has often been used to explain the evangelistic process, but I think it says much more. These verses describe people who talk to other people, trying to explain something to them. We often call that "teaching."

This very familiar passage uses a single metaphor—farming. Jesus called it the parable of the sower.

Interesting, isn't it, that a farming metaphor applies so nicely to what teachers do when we add the word "nurture." Wouldn't you say that nurture is a very good word to describe Christian education? Christian parents nurture their children at home. Pastors nurture congregations in the local church. Christian school teachers and seminary professors nurture students in class. Nurturing. Yet nurturing is not first an educational term, but rather carries a strong mothering connotation. We see its use as well as a botanical term. Our passage gives us four focal points—the farmer, the seed, the ground and the crop—each affording further insight into the communication process.

THE FARMER

Again Jesus began to teach by the lake. The crowd that gathered around him was so large that he got into a boat and sat in it out on the lake, while all the people were along the shore at the water's edge. He taught them many things by parables, and in his teaching said: "Listen! A farmer went out to sow his seed." (Mark 4:1–3)

In our parable, the farmer is Jesus. He describes Himself as one who communicates the truth of the Word. He seems to say to the disciples, "You are also farmers and, insofar as you sow the seed, you are like me." So in application, the farmer represents all those who plant and nurture in the name of the Lord Jesus.

In the sense, then, that educators are "farmers" in the classroom, we represent the activity of God toward our students. Notice that the seed doesn't ask to be sown, nor does the ground say, "Here, sow on me!" Jesus, the farmer, the educator—each takes the initiating step in the nurturing process. Jesus, as God in the flesh, knew the people to whom He spoke; He was prepared ahead of time for the task of self-sacrificial love.

A good farmer, one whose crop comes in with exuberant abundance, studies the horticultural process, knows the fields, rotates the crops, and stays abreast of the new developments with fertilizers and pest control. As teachers, with the same hope of overflowing return, we must also study our pupils, remain aware of the latest research on education, keep our own training fresh and up-to-date. A stale teacher has no more chance of reproducing than a lazy farmer who ruins the land by neglect and ill use.

THE SEED

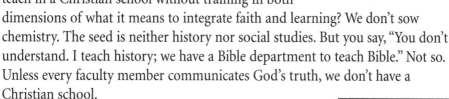

As he was scattering the seed, some fell along the path, and the birds came and ate it up. The farmer sows the word. (Mark 4:4, 14)

The Seed Is the Word

"The farmer sows the word." Bible focus must occupy central place in the curriculum of a Christian school. We plant truth. How can one teach in a Christian school without training in both dimensions of what it means to integrate faith and learning? We don't sow chemistry. The seed is neither history nor social studies. But you say, "You don't understand. I teach history; we have a Bible department to teach Bible." Not so. Unless every faculty member communicates God's truth, we don't have a Christian school.

The country of South Africa has mandated by law that religion be taught in public schools. Such courses are taught side by side: chemistry, history, social studies and religion. Does that make a Christian school? Never. The seed is the Word. Regardless of the training you have at any level of your particular discipline, you must understand God's Word; you must understand Christian theology to be a Christian school teacher. I happen to believe that requires formal study. Not everybody in the movement would agree.

> "Unless every faculty member communicates God's truth, we don't have a Christian school."

The Seed Appears Dead While It Still Has Life in It

The farmer takes that little grain of corn, puts it into the ground and amazing things happen. It's a constant reaffirmation of the principle of resurrection. I studied Latin in junior high (if you can picture that) and as junior high students will do, we wrote graffiti all over our books. One poem we wrote looks like this: "Latin is a dead language, as dead as dead can be. First it killed the Romans and now it's killing me." But Latin is alive and well—if you know the language, you recognize it in Spanish, Italian, German, French and English.

The seed is like that. You say, "Well, maybe if I were a Bible teacher. Then I could believe that even though my junior high students don't respond, life continues in the seed so I keep spreading it." No, not just the Bible teacher; all truth is God's truth. If we integrate Biblical truth with whatever we teach, then we teach truth.

We could expand this into a discussion of natural revelation and special revelation, but let's not get that fussy about it. Let's just say that one of the interesting parallels between farming and teaching shows us that life resides in both seed and truth; we sow and sometimes don't see results for months or even years. That provides us with both the problems and blessings of teaching. We wrestle with the lack of immediate change in our schoolchildren. Then five years later one of them walks into your room and says, "Remember me?" You remember him all right; you wanted to shoot him more than once. Then he begins to tell you how God has changed his life because you taught truth in the classroom and he heard it.

The Seed Was Given to the Disciples

We know that the seed was given to the disciples for them to sow in turn. What trust Jesus placed in these people! With a message of such importance, one would think that Jesus should pick only the best and the brightest, the most highly qualified, those with the most prestigious credentials. Yet, when we look, we see people pulled off the street, ordinary people who fished and taxed and sat under trees and battled hot tempers and unbelief. Not a born leader in the crowd—clear evidence that leadership skills reflect learned behavior, not inborn traits.

But you may say it was experience. No, Jesus spoke this parable only six months into His ministry. What seems to be at stake here is perseverance and willingness. Remember the farming metaphor; keep putting seed into the ground until something grows. Just stay with it.

In 1895, missionaries of the Africa Inland Mission first penetrated the interior of that country. They had served on the coasts, but they decided the time had come to go inland. They sent the first group of

"Although I am an English teacher, it is the Word of God that I must first sow in the lives of my students. Even though I love to teach literature, writing skills and grammar, only the principles from God's Word will truly help my students as they walk the pathway of life." ~ Debbie, Iowa

missionaries to pierce the interior of Africa—they pierced and they died. They sent in a second group of missionaries—they pierced and they died. The missionaries on the coasts cabled the States (obviously I'm describing something happening over years), "Send us more recruits; send us more missionaries." A third group came, packing their belongings in their own caskets, assuming from the day they left home that they would die on the field.

An amazing story, but don't push the metaphor too far. I'm not saying they will carry you out of sixth grade one of these days and that will be it! I'm just making the point that the farmer keeps sowing the seed, though it may seem lifeless and inconsequential, because she is committed to what she believes God wants to her to do.

The Ground

As he was scattering the seed, some fell along the path, and the birds came and ate it up. Some fell on rocky places, where it did not have much soil. It sprang up quickly, because the soil was shallow. But when the sun came up, the plants were scorched, and they withered because they had no root. Other seed fell among thorns, which grew up and choked the plants, so that they did not bear grain. Still other seed fell on good soil. It came up, grew and produced a crop, multiplying thirty, sixty, or even a hundred times. (Mark 4:4–8)

On a Path

Four kinds of soil. First, soil like a path—hard, beaten down by lots of feet pounding it through the years. Perhaps some of your students seem like that. And some have been beaten down, perhaps by their own parents, by other teachers, or even by their own sense of insecurity. As we sow the seed, we know that not all of it will fall on good ground. That's the point of the parable.

In the Bible story, the path probably represents the Pharisees, among the brightest skilled intellectuals of Jesus' day. But the hardness of their hearts indicated unreceptiveness to the seed. Some kids will never get it. They will go all the way through your school and never change. They will graduate as hard as they matriculated and cause grief to you and to many others as well. Yet Jesus does not seem to begrudge that some of the seed, the Word of God, will fall on that hard ground. He sows generously, and whosoever will may come. Let us be equally as generous as we sow truth in the classroom, even to those who act as though they walk surrounded by a plastic circle, so protected by its hardness that nothing seems to penetrate. Perhaps somewhere a crack will appear.

Some will remember a popular story from many years ago, *A Tree Grows in Brooklyn.* This warm and loving novel told of a girl growing up in a slum environment with everything against her. She flourished nonetheless, gaining an education as she developed into innocent womanhood. Hard ground to the outside eye, but the will to live and bloom superseded the circumstances.

In Rocky Places

The parable contains no percentage, but three out of four kinds of ground have problems. The rocky soil serves as a good warning to practice discernment when working with students. Sometimes quick results indicate neither lasting power nor real depth in the spiritual life. We've all had experience with those who quickly learn the ability to spout the "right" answers, who quickly master Christian jargon and sound deeply spiritual. Yet when we put them to the test, expecting solid decisions and faithful work, we experience disappointment with the performance. Apparently rejection goes with the job; perhaps if we expect it, we will be more prepared to face it without severe discouragement.

Among Thorns

Notice that the thorns only appeared after the seed was sown. The parable tells us the seed fell there and grew up, but the stronger thorns choked the plants. That will happen to some of your students and some of mine. But as a good farmer, and as a wise nurturer, you know that, although you don't see thorns at sowing time, they will come. Keep in touch with reality. Never expect too much lest you build yourself into a corner of disappointment and despair.

> "Our schools are about sowing the seed in good ground so that student lives can change."

Into Good Soil

How much good soil do you need to keep teaching? How much response will keep you in the classroom? I deal with church staff people all the time who ask similar questions. What kind of response must I have to stay at this church? About 10 percent growth a year? At least some phase of a building program every five years? Changes in the missions budget? More income? Greater salary? More amens? What will it take? How much good soil do you need to keep teaching?

I'm told that one square meter of rich soil may contain more than one billion organisms busily producing an environment. What kind of good ground did Jesus need? Not the crowds. They left as quickly as they came. The disciples? Where were they at the time of the Cross?

By modern standards, Jesus failed in everything He claimed He wanted to do. A modern pastor investing three-and-a-half years and producing only what the Lord left behind would, by usual standards, be considered wasting his time. But we can't judge ministry by the measures of business and industry. We don't deal with bottom-line management; we focus on changes in people's lives. The issue is not school size, athletic success, or even academic excellence, as much as we desire all these. Our schools are about sowing the seed in good ground so that student lives can change.

THE CROP

Some people are like seed along the path, where the word is sown. As soon as they hear it, Satan comes and takes away the word that was sown in them. Others, like seed sown on rocky places, hear the word and at once receive it with joy. But since they have no root, they last only a short time. When trouble or persecution comes because of the word, they quickly fall away. Still others, like seed sown among thorns, hear the word; but the worries of this life, the deceitfulness of wealth and the desires for other things come in and choke the word, making it unfruitful. Others, like seed sown on good soil, hear the word, accept it, and produce a crop—thirty, sixty or even a hundred times what was sown. (Mark 4:15–20)

As we continue to compare Christian teaching to farming, we see that surely we can learn to expect four kinds of crops.

Reality of Satan

The reality of Satan does not require constant exorcism and finding demons behind every bush. The parable tells us what happens when the seed lands on the path—Satan snatches it away. Not some kind of distant, vague force unrelated to what we do, Satan constantly battles with us in the classroom every time we try to sow the seed. We can go into our classrooms conscious of the

Lord's presence—and we should—but we dare not underestimate the adversary, ready to snatch away the seed that falls on the path.

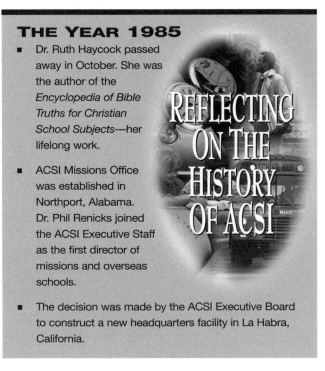

THE YEAR 1985

- Dr. Ruth Haycock passed away in October. She was the author of the *Encyclopedia of Bible Truths for Christian School Subjects*—her lifelong work.

- ACSI Missions Office was established in Northport, Alabama. Dr. Phil Renicks joined the ACSI Executive Staff as the first director of missions and overseas schools.

- The decision was made by the ACSI Executive Board to construct a new headquarters facility in La Habra, California.

REFLECTING ON THE HISTORY OF ACSI

Superficiality of Commitment

Now we return to the seed that falls in rocky places. It springs up and we get all excited. Something seems to grow, but it does not. Trouble burns it away. Evangelical Christianity today suffers from lack of commitment. People just do not want to follow through. Great starters, poor finishers. A recent survey found that 90 percent of Americans believe in God. Unfortunately, it has minimal effect on their lives. The researchers wrote:

> . . . when we asked how people make up their minds on issues of right and wrong, we found that they simply do not turn to God or religion to help them decide about

the seminal or moral issues of the day. For most people, religion plays virtually no role in shaping their opinions on a long list of important public questions.[1]

If we can identify that problem in the church at large, surely as teachers we better expect superficiality of commitment.

Commonalty of Worldliness

Remember the third kind of ground? Thorns. What did the thorns represent? The text is clear: "Still others, like seed sown among thorns, hear the word; but the worries of this life, the deceitfulness of wealth and the desires for other things come in and choke the word" (*vv*. 18–19).

Can affluence and Christianity mix? Are not all of us prone to worries of some sort? Have any managed to completely free themselves from desires? The parable does not suggest that these things do not exist in the life of one who responds to the Seed of Life. Instead, we learn that these things, when unchecked, will bring about unfruitfulness. Let's return to the farmer—a good farmer will keep abreast of the thorns and keep them in check so they don't crowd out the crop. A nurturing teacher and educator keeps an alert eye for those who find themselves too tangled by today's thorns.

Howard Hendricks, my colleague at Dallas Theological Seminary, once served as chaplain for the Dallas Cowboys. Howie was on the practice field with the Dallas Cowboys during spring training back in 1985, standing next to Tom Landry. He said, "Tom, you've been coaching for almost as many years as I've been teaching. What changes have you seen in professional football players since you started?"

To which Coach Landry responded, "Today's players are more gifted and less disciplined than ever before."

I wonder if we could take the word "players" out, replacing it with "students," perhaps adding "distracted." Would we be right?

Vitality of Teaching

With all this bad soil, one would think the disciples might leave saying, "What's the use?" But the parable ends on a positive note. You throw seed into the good soil and it explodes—"thirty, sixty, even a hundred times what was sown." Jesus, the Son of God, could say to His disciples, "Greater things than I have done, you will do" (John 14:12).

What do you suppose they thought? I can see them turn to one another and say, "Did I hear that right? Is this really what He said? What does He mean by that?"

Why not take that passage literally? They went to places He never saw. They ministered far more years than He did. They led thousands to the truth. I think Jesus meant what He said. Teaching is a ministry of multiplication.

Interestingly, the difference in the crop does not depend on the seed. Nothing in the parable says, "You get good seed and bad seed. If you should acquire a handful of bad seed, then you are going to . . ." No, all the seed in the parable was good. We assume the farmer has nothing but good seed. You can make up your own parable and put in bad seed, but none shows up in this one.

Second, the difference in the crop is not due to the method of scattering. We could say, "The dumb farmer throws his seed where it can't grow. He ought to know not to put it on the path, the rocky places, or where the thorns will come up." But a first-century farmer deliberately let the

> To what does Jesus attribute the difference? First, to student response—the kind of ground.... Ultimately, of course, the crop is due to God's grace."

wind take seed wherever it went. To be sure, when we sow the truth we know that every place will not give forth valuable grain, fruit and plants. But certainly we cannot fault the method.

To what does Jesus attribute the difference? First, to student response—the kind of ground. Somebody needs to be preparing the ground. Somehow we've got to get beyond the boundaries of the opening bell and back to the parents. As we enlist their support in preparing the ground, the seed has a better chance of growing.

Ultimately, of course, the crop is due to God's grace. God uses our faithful sowing, nurturing, communication of truth to produce fruitful, verdant and vital new life. What can we say about Christian teaching except that God produces miracles through His Word and by His grace.

ENDNOTES

1. James Patterson and Peter Kim, *The Day America Told the Truth* (New York: Prentice Hall Press, 1991), 199.

CHAPTER NINE
1986
THAT CHILDREN MIGHT KNOW THE WORKS OF GOD

their children:
6 That the generation to come
might know them, even the
children which should be born;
should arise and declare
to their children:

Psalm 78:1-8

I n a provocative book entitled *Children Without Childhood*, Marie Winn identifies what she names enemies of Western culture: the sexual revolution; proliferation of television; increase in divorce and single parenting; and the forcing of children into adulthood too soon.[1] Our society prides itself on its love of children and its comprehensive educational system; yet an increasing number of voices suggest that our national concern for children may be just a facade.

In May 1984, *Christianity Today* carried an article by Rodney Clapp warning about the attitude of society, particularly in this decade.

> There are many signs that children are increasingly less appreciated in our society and that childhood as we know it is threatened with change to the point of extinction. The boundary protecting children is no concrete, biological wall, as unchallengeable as the law of gravity. It is a thin, cultural veil, gradually raised in the past for good reason. It tears easily. And anyone who listens can hear it ripping.[2]

The Bible has a great deal to say about our families and how we teach children the truth of God's Word. Those of us who teach in Christian schools at any level would do well to remember we teach the children of God. Like Anna in the service of the king of Siam, we teach the King's children. This dramatic psalm deals with that responsibility and identifies several requirements or commitments such teachers must have.

"We teach the King's children."

Psalm 78 probably dates from the time of the divided monarchy, perhaps during the life of the prophet Hosea. Its seventy-two musical verses were written to warn worshippers at Jerusalem (southern kingdom) not to fall into apostasy and ruin as did their brothers to the north. Repeatedly we see the contrast between the sin of Israel and the unending mercy of God. The commitment of the psalmist parallels our own: "Our children must hear what our fathers have told us so that they may be faithful to the Lord."

COMMITMENT TO CONTENT

O my people, hear my teaching;
*   listen to the words of my mouth.*
I will open my mouth in parables,
*   I will utter hidden things, things from of old—*
what we have heard and known,
*   what our fathers have told us.*
(Psalm 78:1–3)

A saph was a Levite, a member of a family of singers who assisted in temple worship. This particular psalm expresses wisdom or insight. Notice his emphasis on content in the first three verses where he uses the words "teaching," "words," "parables," "heard," "known" and the expression "told us."

Many adults today show a tendency to worship at the academic altar. We want our children to have the best education and urge them to do well in school all the time. Education, seen in terms of acquisition of knowledge in order to gain economic power, serves as the end goal, beyond character development and healthy spiritual life. Others, however, deny the relevancy of education and even laugh at the idea of pastors studying in a seminary. They seem to fear that the development of an active intellectual life will lead to denial of basic truths. As usual, both extremes probably reflect error. Asaph avoids confusion by centering his emphasis on content—something specific must be taught.

The psalm focuses on the centrality of the Bible. The various words we noted above represent the Scriptures known and used at the time Asaph wrote these words. Today we have much more of the Bible, but we still hold Scripture as central to all that we teach. We want to avoid the extreme of intellectual idolatry, the concept that knowledge in and of itself brings anyone closer to God and to holy living. Remember, Christian teaching finds its primary role in spiritual maturation, not the accumulation of information. We do not deny the importance of the works of Plato, Beethoven and Einstein, but they do not represent the central focus for Christian teaching. God reserves that place for His Word.

Notice too that the authority for teaching has been passed on to the teacher by someone else. Asaph says, "I will utter hidden things, things from of old—what we have heard and known, what our fathers have told us." Authority wraps itself in the content handed down from grandparents to parents to children. Of course, not every family functions that way since not all grandparents and parents are believers. But this displays God's ideal. We see here a reminder to protect the spiritual heritage of our families by making sure that serious teaching goes on in each generation.

> "Remember, Christian teaching finds its primary role in spiritual maturation, not the accumulation of information."

Consider for a moment the struggles that some adopted people face as they move into adulthood. They have been cut off from their genetic family history; they may experience a sense of lostness, of detachment from any real roots. This determination to find those roots may push a lengthy and time-consuming investigation. The psalmist gives the mandate to keep our spiritual history alive, to remind our young people of their heritage all the way through the ages.

Perhaps that is why God created Christian schools. One could wish that a godly family complemented by a Bible-teaching church would provide all the spiritual instruction any child or young person could possibly need. Many of us as parents, however, discovered early on that this iniquitous culture, with its disdain for the past and validation only of present experience, forms a frightening foe. We need all the help we can possibly get!

> *"Woe to you experts in the law, because you have taken away the key to knowledge. You yourselves have not entered, and you have hindered those who were entering."* (Luke 11:52)

As teachers, we must ask if we open the doors to our heritage or keep them tightly shut by making the studies confusing or boring or unapproachable. This mysterious verse in the gospel of Luke ought to haunt the days and nights of every teacher. These experts in the law were professional students of the Old Testament, not civil or criminal attorneys. The difference between Pharisees and religious lawyers in Jesus' day might be similar to the difference between pastors and professors today. The Pharisees served a religious party (denomination) and the experts in the law served a profession. Apparently Jesus considered their spiritual responsibility to be equal.

These teachers should have provided the key to understanding Old Testament content. But not only had they themselves not entered into the real meaning of those texts, they had taken away motivation and comprehension from those who really wanted to know what God had said. As Matthew put it, they "shut the kingdom of heaven in men's faces" (Matthew 23:13). Leon Morris writes of these Bible experts:

> "The psalmist gives the mandate to keep our spiritual history alive, to remind our young people of their heritage all the way through the ages."

> They turned the Bible into a book of obscurities, a bundle of riddles. Only the experts could understand it. And the experts themselves were so pleased and preoccupied with the mysteries they had manufactured that they missed the wonderful things that God was saying. They neither entered themselves nor allowed others to enter. There were ordinary people on their way to the knowledge of God until their teachers turned them away.[3]

The psalmist tells us to utter things hidden from of old. For the rest of the psalm, he recounts the history of Israel in a powerful and easy-to-remember poetic structure. He opens the doors and invites us in. What a model to follow!

COMMITMENT TO COMMUNICATION

We will not hide them from their children;
*   we will tell the next generation*
the praiseworthy deeds of the Lord,
*   his power, and the wonders he has done.*
He decreed statutes for Jacob
*   and established the law in Israel,*
which he commanded our forefathers
*   to teach their children.*
(Psalm 78:4–5)

Once again the spotlight falls upon family responsibility. Asaph could not be more clear: "We will tell the next generation the praiseworthy deeds of the Lord." The message, open and clear, declares that children don't have to guess what their parents hold true. Today's more popular mode allows children to make their own ethical and moral choices. The whole values clarification movement urges children to select the best among alternatives, not to embrace the absolute morality which may have been taught by their parents from the Bible.

What has God done? Asaph reminds us that "He decreed statutes for Jacob and established the law in Israel, which he commanded our forefathers to teach their children." We might add, He has told us of the birth, life, death and resurrection of Jesus Christ; the development of the church; detailed commandments regarding the Christian life; and a great deal of prophecy yet to be fulfilled. How dare we refuse or even carelessly neglect teaching such truth to our students!

God wills the communication of His truth to children in the family and the Christian school. Jesus Himself exemplified such teaching even though His own disciples thought it improper.

> "He has told us of the birth, life, death and resurrection of Jesus Christ; the development of the church; detailed commandments regarding the Christian life; and a great deal of prophecy yet to be fulfilled. How dare we refuse or even carelessly neglect teaching such truth to our students!"

> *Then little children were brought to Jesus for him to place his hands on them and pray for them. But the disciples rebuked those who brought them.*
>
> *Jesus said, "Let the little children come to me, and do not hinder them, for the kingdom of heaven belongs to such as these." When he had placed his hands on them, he went on from there.* (Matthew 19:13–15)

The kingdom of heaven may ultimately belong to little children, but we are not a society that cares much to make that kingdom living available now. *Newsweek* magazine report that, in 1993, "there were 1 million confirmed cases of [child] abuse and neglect . . . an estimated 462,000 children were in substitute care . . . 42 percent of the 1,300 kids who died as a result of abuse last year had previously been reported to child-protection agencies."[4]

What do we communicate to our children? That God is unloving, uncaring, capricious? Or that God has a history of redemptive activity toward those He loves and has committed Himself? By understanding and communicating the long-term history of God's actions, we may help our young people build a

"The psalmist knew the importance of relaying to the next generation the wonderful things that God had done for His people. Unfortunately, today's students no longer see any connection between their lives and their spiritual heritage."

~ Don, New Hampshire

framework for belief that will carry them through the difficult times.

COMMITMENT TO CONTINUATION

So the next generation would know them,
  even the children yet to be born,
  and they in turn would tell their children.
Then they would put their trust in God
  and would not forget his deeds
  but would keep his commands.
(Psalm 78:6–7)

You may have heard about the second grader who brought home a report card that didn't meet his parent's expectations. After dinner Dad said, "Son, we are going to have to do something about these grades."

To which the boy replied, "We can't, Dad, they're in ink."

God will not allow Christians to shift familial accountability to the church, Christian school or other organizations and agencies. Teachers are mentors, role models, advisors and friends to their students. But in those various roles we serve as bench players—substitutes for parents. Through all the years of parental relationship, God expects teaching to be one of their major responsibilities.

Parents or teachers who teach God's Word to children must have adequate preparation. Remember the old Nike shoe commercial? Moses Malone (then with the Philadelphia 76ers) stands alone in an empty gymnasium throwing the ball up to the backboard and catching it—throwing it and catching it, throwing it and catching it—over and over. We hear no words until Moses finally turns toward the camera and says, "The way I figure it, before you shoot the ball you've got to get the ball." Teachers who do not know God's Word and do not prepare for their tasks will find themselves inadequate and frustrated when trying to carry out the God-given command to insure that children know the works of God.

All this sounds quite idealistic. Words of the psalmist in verses 6 and 7 picture a *Saturday Evening Post* family, hands folded around the table after dinner, collectively intent on growing in God's righteousness. In reality, both parents and teachers fail with discouraging regularity. Yet those failures provide magnificent opportunities for future achievement.

Many of the finest business writers of our day indicate that the old adage "Success breeds success" lacks veracity. One ought to say, "Failure breeds success" because only failure can provide the learning experience we need.

Urban Hilger, Jr., president of the Dalmo-Victor Division of the Singer Company tells about his first day on the ski slopes. He skied all day long and didn't fall once so he proudly

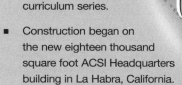

THE YEAR 1986

- ACSI began to "recruit" teachers for overseas schools at ACSI teacher conventions.

- The first "statement of purpose" article was drafted by ACSI as the starting point for its nationwide curriculum goals project. This was the first step to the development of the many ACSI curriculum series.

- Construction began on the new eighteen thousand square foot ACSI Headquarters building in La Habra, California.

- The first European Conference of Christian Educators was held at Black Forest Academy in Kandern, Germany.

REFLECTING ON THE HISTORY OF ACSI

announced that achievement to his instructor at the end of the day. The instructor's response shocked Hilger: "Personally, Urban, I think you had a lousy day. If you're not falling, you're not learning."

What were your most profound learning experiences? When you eased through a new task without any significant error or when you had to redo and experiment and keep coming back in order to finish it properly? Yes, we want our students—and ourselves—to learn our spiritual heritage which can build motivation to keep God's commands. But we will all fail, and Psalm 78 speaks as much about the never-tiring grace of God as it does about obedience. Failure and defeat need not be equated.

Experimentation is crucial for all of us. We are rather like that novice lion tamer being interviewed:

"I understand your father was also a lion tamer," the reporter queried.
"Yes, he was," the man replied.
"Do you actually put your head into the lion's mouth?"
"I did it only once," said the new lion tamer, "to look for Dad."

> "We want our students—and ourselves—to learn our spiritual heritage which can build motivation to keep God's commands."

We want to build upon our successes and learn from our failures. In fact, that is precisely what the final verse tells us.

COMMITMENT TO CONTRAST

> They would not be like their forefathers—
>   a stubborn and rebellious generation,
> whose hearts were not loyal to God,
>   whose spirits were not faithful to him.
> (Psalm 78:8)

In the final verse of our passage, Asaph and God's Holy Spirit who guided him in writing this psalm point out that families do go bad, and the chain of teaching God's truth does not always stand unbroken from generation to generation. In fact, this psalm seems intent on revival, getting back to God's initial intent rather than imitating the sins and failures of recent "forefathers." Notice that all the sins of our verse reflect behaviors quite common in our society today. Parents and teachers must work to produce reverse qualities which, like all Christian standards, tend to be countercultural. Asaph bemoans the recollection that these forefathers were stubborn, rebellious, disloyal and faithless. On the other hand, God's children must be flexible, obedient, loyal and faithful.

In the book of Matthew, our Lord points out the vulnerability of children and how much the heavenly Father wishes to protect them. In that quality, *we* are to be like *them—the pedagogical model in reverse.*

> He called a little child and had him stand among them. And he said: "I tell you the truth, unless you change and become like little children, you will never enter the kingdom of heaven. Therefore, whoever humbles himself like this child is the greatest in the kingdom of heaven.
> And whoever welcomes a little child like this in my name welcomes me. But if anyone causes one of these little ones who believe in me to sin, it would be better for him to have a large millstone hung around his neck and to be drowned in the depths of the sea. (Matthew 18:2–6)

The countercultural stance today mandates a strong return to the protection of children, to the maintenance of their innocence. I do not suggest that children remain foolishly naive, but that we stop encouraging them to sin by such constant exposure to violence, sex, and brutality. Can teachers do all that?

No, we cannot. But the Christian school can provide an environment of loving and joyful communication of truth in such a manner that it exposes the degradation of nontruth to the light of holiness.

Teaching God's children—what a glorious task, what a fulfilling responsibility! We must love our students; proclaim the gospel to our students; and protect those students whom God has called us to tend as a shepherd does little lambs. Parents and teachers of the world, unite in response to God's Word in Psalm 78.

ENDNOTES

1. Marie Winn, *Children Without Childhood* (New York: Penguin, 1984).
2. Rodney Clapp, "Vanishing Childhood, Part I," *Christianity Today* (May 1984): 12.
3. Leon Morris, "Luke," *Tyndale New Testament Commentaries* (Grand Rapids: Eerdmans, 1974), 207.
4. Michele Ingrassia and John McCormick, "Why Leave Children with Bad Parents?" *Newsweek* (25 April 1994): 53.

CHAPTER TEN

DESIRE THE WORD AND GROW

all evil speakings,
2 As newborn babes, desire
the sincere milk of the word,
that ye may grow thereby:
3 If so be ye have tasted that
Lord is gracious.

1 Peter 2:1-3

When we view life in the perspective of eternity, salvation is only the beginning. From that starting point, Christians begin to build a life in Christ, growing much like physical children. By design the Bible uses the metaphor of infancy and childhood to describe a person young in the faith. Our key verse comes from 1 Peter 2.

Therefore, rid yourselves of all malice and all deceit, hypocrisy, envy, and slander of every kind. Like newborn babies, crave pure spiritual milk, so that by it you may grow up in your salvation, now that you have tasted that the Lord is good. (1 Peter 2:1–3)

The first ten verses of 1 Peter 2 flow directly out of chapter 1. The word "therefore" points to the salvation experience as Peter reminds young Christians to set aside the past and to grow in the present. Like education, sanctification is a developmental process. The reference to "spiritual milk" clearly refers to God's Word since new Christians, like new babies, can only grow if they eat correctly.

Notice how important experience becomes in all of this. I heard about a lawyer for a hit-and-run driver who argued that the injured pedestrian must have been careless because his client had been driving for twenty years without an accident. To which the prosecutor replied, "If experience is the issue here, let it be shown that my client has been walking without accident for fifty years."

Silly, of course. But it points up the idea that years of experience in either walking or driving are pointless unless accompanied by growth and progress—which implies learning and dumps this entire passage right back in our pedagogical laps.

Before I go any further let me offer a confession, thereby releasing the burden of writing this chapter. The outline I offer here is as old as my ministry since it dates back to the first or second sermon I ever preached. I know, you wonder about all those years of growth and development. But in fact, built upon words in the text itself, the outline is so simple I feel constrained not to change it. Kindergartners could memorize it in a minute, Peter reminds his readers in these first two chapters that developing Christians must *know, grow* and *show*.

Nurture, a word we have discussed earlier, becomes key in such a discussion. Maturing students in Christian education do not drop like a candy bar to the bottom of the vending machine when we deposit the seventy-five cents. As important as *product* is in our business, *process* may be even more important. That's one reason why our nation waits in frightening anticipation to see the products of the current day-care crisis.

> The figures are staggering. Ten million children under the age of six have two working parents or a single parent who supports the family. By 1995 two-thirds of all preschoolers will have mothers in the work force. And yet, in 1986, there were only 40,000 day-care centers and 105,000 licensed day-care homes watching over 2.1 million children. Every day, millions of other children are sent to unregulated facilities, where the quality of care they get varies widely.[1]

Will these children be adequately nurtured? I do not question the motives of working mothers—economic survival must be considered. I question instead

THE YEAR 1987

- ACSI moved into its new headquarters in La Habra, California.

- Joseph Smith retired from ACSI staff after serving for seventeen years with CACS, WACS and ACSI. Mr. Smith was the first CACS staff person, at the director level, hired by Dr. Paul Kienel.

- Combined ACSI teacher convention attendance exceeded twenty-five thousand for the first time.

- The division of California, Nevada and Hawaii into two ACSI regions was finalized.

- The First International Boarding Conference was held in Quito, Ecuador. Dr. Philip Renicks was chairman.

- The first Prefield Orientation for missionary teachers and boarding home parents was sponsored by ACSI, Interaction and Missionary Internship.

REFLECTING ON THE HISTORY OF ACSI

the long-term effect on these children in a society that does not give high value to those who perform the incomparably valuable task of nurturing our children. The quality/quantity time debate will rage for years to come. In the meantime, the moment-by-moment guidance and love for these children may prove inadequate. What kind of damage repair

must the Christian school expect in the coming years? What are the basics that we may have to reteach rather than expect already implanted?

GROWING CHRISTIANS MUST KNOW

Of course, when we hear a statement like our heading, we simply ask, "Know what?" Certainly foundational aspects of doctrine. Peter argues we have been freed from an empty lifestyle to experience God's truth firsthand. He doesn't leave us wondering what that might be, but tells us it is the truth of the atonement (1 Peter 1:18–20); the truth of the Resurrection (*v.* 21); and the truth of Christian living (*v.* 17). Here's the text.

> *Since you call on a Father who judges each man's work impartially, live your lives as strangers here in reverent fear. For you know that it was not with perishable things such as silver or gold that you were redeemed from the empty way of life handed down to you from your forefathers, but with the precious blood of Christ, a lamb without blemish or defect. He was chosen before the creation of the world, but was revealed in these last times for your sake. Through him you believe in God, who raised him from the dead and glorified him, and so your faith and hope are in God.* (1 Peter 1:17–21)

The first chapter goes on to tell us that knowledge should produce obedience in a crucial area.

> *Now that you have purified yourselves by obeying the truth so that you have sincere love for your brothers, love one another deeply, from the heart. For you have been born again, not of perishable seed, but of imperishable, through the living and enduring word of God.* (1 Peter 1:22–23)

In the Christian life, knowledge produces obedience through love. Icebergs and churches are both beautiful, but in very different ways. One has a cold hard beauty we can admire from a distance or in pictures. The beauty of a church emanates from a warmth of love and demonstration of grace among its people.

This love arises from a pure heart and focuses primarily on fellow believers. Surely other places in Scripture remind us we must love those outside the faith as well, but that is not the focus here. Obviously then love of fellow teachers and of our students reflects our obedience to God.

But verse 23 reminds us that we also love simply because we have been born again. New believers turn from the negative to the positive, from starvation to nourishment, from the morass of sin to the milk of Scripture. In order for that to be possible, they must know God's Word.

> "Love of fellow teachers and of our students reflects our obedience to God."

The birth comes through the living and abiding Word of God, a reference both to the Bible (God's Word in revelation) and to the Holy Spirit who lives Christ's life in us (God's revelation through incarnation). Peter's quotation from Isaiah 40:6–8 (1 Peter 1:24–25) seems especially fitting for pilgrim Christians in a pagan world. All flesh will perish; only the Word of God will endure forever. What must growing Christians know? Doubtless many things, but at the core—God's Holy Word.

That's a tall order—theologians spend lifetimes uncovering the depths of Scripture truth. You have other things you must do: prepare lesson plans for your particular grade or subject areas, create and grade evaluation instruments, attend faculty gatherings, meet family responsibilities, care for your physical needs. Yet as I have emphasized before, if you do not know the Scriptures well enough to give you the confidence to measure accurately so-called "truths" against absolute truth, then you are not adequately prepared to teach in a Christian school.

> "What must growing Christians know? Doubtless many things, but at the core—God's Holy Word."

The very day I write this chapter, *The Dallas Morning News* carried a story on the front page of the business section. Apparently a public relations firm conducted a survey of 311 "Fortune 1000" presidents and vice presidents asking them what person most influenced them as business leaders in running their companies during 1993. Doubtless the surveyors expected names like Peter Drucker, Lee Iaccoca or Bill Clinton to appear. The most mentioned name was Dallas Cowboys' head coach Jimmy Johnson and two of the other top five were New York Knicks' coach Pat Riley and (of all things) Madonna!

When asked which part of the paper they read first, these high-powered, overpaid, overworked executives said the sports page (32%), lifestyles (21%), front page (18%), horoscopes (16%), comics (10%) and finally, business pages (2%).[2]

Despite their exalted positions, one could hardly be faulted for concluding that these executives do not read the right things. And when we view education from the vantage point of 1 Peter 1, we might very well conclude that many Christian schools may be emphasizing with time and money something other than the central priority. As in business, so in Christian education, the main thing is to keep the main thing the main thing.

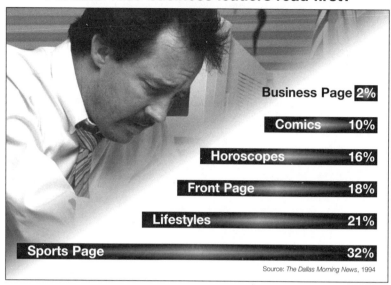

Which part of the newspaper do Fortune 1000 business leaders read first?

Business Page 2%
Comics 10%
Horoscopes 16%
Front Page 18%
Lifestyles 21%
Sports Page 32%

Source: *The Dallas Morning News*, 1994

GROWING CHRISTIANS MUST GROW

Therefore, rid yourselves of all malice and all deceit, hypocrisy, envy, and slander of every kind. Like newborn babies, crave pure spiritual milk, so that by it you may grow up in your salvation, now that you have tasted that the Lord is good. (1 Peter 2:1–3)

Those who use the Word properly, Peter says, will grow in righteousness, drawing away from the five sins of attitude and speech which he lists here.

The Bible contains numerous "vice lists" and this one consists of malice, deceit, hypocrisy, envy and slander. Putting those five in a slightly different framework, we could say that the growing Christian puts behind her wicked ill will, deliberate dishonesty, pretend piety, resentful discontent and vengeful lies. Then she can move on to maturity in the pure use of God's Word.

"Maturity is the ability to live with your child even though he is just like you."
~ Sam Levinson

What is maturity? According to humorist Sam Levinson, maturity is the ability to live with your child even though he is just like you. Perhaps. But real

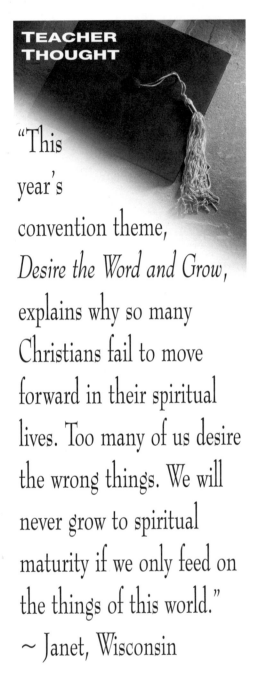

"This year's convention theme, *Desire the Word and Grow,* explains why so many Christians fail to move forward in their spiritual lives. Too many of us desire the wrong things. We will never grow to spiritual maturity if we only feed on the things of this world."

~ Janet, Wisconsin

maturity comes from knowledge plus experience and it impacts our lives in numerous different ways. Forming Christians must continue to grow in righteousness, in maturity and in consistent spirituality. Let's take a look at verses 4 and 5.

As you come to him, the living Stone—rejected by men but chosen by God and precious to him—you also, like living stones, are being built into a spiritual house to be a holy priesthood, offering spiritual sacrifices acceptable to God through Jesus Christ. (1 Peter 2:4–5)

The agendas of our lives and schools must make room for the priorities of a passage like this and urgency is required.

> They say procrastination is
> The cause of all my sorrow;
> I don't know what that big word means
> But I'll look it up tomorrow.

As a theme, maturity surfaces frequently in these chapters. Perhaps because it so clearly forms a major portion of what God has called us to do. Or perhaps it stems from the fact that many people find immaturity humorous and tend to overlook its frightening consequences.

To be sure, among young children immaturity is funny. Their answers (as every kindergarten teacher knows) are often far more amusing than contrived adult comedy. Somewhere I ran across the following children's quiz on religion; perhaps you have seen it.

Who was Noah's Wife? Joan of Ark.
Which is the fifth commandment? Humor thy father and mother.
Where does the Pope live? In a vacuum.
What is God like? Like grampa sitting on a cloud.
How many wives should a Christian man have? Only one because Christians believe in monotony.
Who was Lot's wife? A pillar of stone by day and ball of fire at night.

Funny stuff. But not if those were sincere answers on a senior Bible test. In both physical and spiritual realms, everyone has a right to be a baby—for a while. But in the plan of God, growing Christians must continue to grow.

GROWING CHRISTIANS MUST SHOW

But you are a chosen people, a royal priesthood, a holy nation, a people belonging to God, that you may declare the praises of him who called you out of darkness into his wonderful light. Once you were not a people, but now you are the people of God; once you had not received mercy, but now you have received mercy. (1 Peter 2:9–10)

These two verses rise poignantly with theological meaning and we only have space to touch on it ever so quickly. *The Expositor's Bible Commentary* offers a helpful paragraph on the phrases Peter uses at the beginning of verse 9.

The title "Chosen People" stresses God's loving initiative in bringing the church to Himself. "Royal priesthood" may be understood as "a royal house," "a body of priests." . . . Both titles stress the dignity of the church because of its union with Christ. Jesus is King, and all in His "house" belong to a royal house. Calling the church "a body of priests" emphasizes its corporate role in worship, intercession, and ministry. "Holy nation" shows that God has "set apart" the church for His use. The title "a people belonging to God" stresses ownership (cf. Titus 2:14: "A people that are His very own").[3]

> "Christian teachers show the message of the Gospel to students by showing we can relate to one another in consistent loving collegiality."

The middle phrase of verse 9 says that we must declare or show the praise of the One who called us out of darkness into His wonderful light. This word (praise) appears four times in the New Testament and focuses on things like the qualities, excellencies or virtues of God. Peter emphasizes how we Christians reflect the great light of our heavenly Father.

Verse 10 emphasizes family membership. God's people always form a group. Salvation may be individual, but the expression of new life in Christ takes place in groups.

I read about a fellow hanging a 4 x 8 poster at the end of a large room at work. Another employee offered help but he said, "No, I can do it myself." Finally as he wrestled the huge placard up against the wall, the letters announced their message to the room: "Together we can find the answer." Christian teachers show the message of the Gospel to students by showing we can relate to one another in consistent loving collegiality.

To be sure, Christians can learn on their own, and to a lesser extent, develop spiritual formation on their own. But the best growing is done with others and certainly the showing must be done as a corporate entity. Think about it. The familiar "one another" passages in Romans can be expressed only in the context of community. We have two great commandments: to love God and to love one another. How do we become sharpened in our spiritual lives? By gentle admonishments, by speaking the truth in love, by living in such a context that our rough edges are blunted and smoothed by contact with one another.

Verses 11 and 12 form a bridge to the rest of this chapter. Verse 11 tells us to put away evil and verse 12, to live as examples. Actually, verse 12 calls for a "noble lifestyle," the shining reflection of that corporate demonstration of God's grace in a darkened world. In Peter's day, Christians were accused of being disloyal to the State, of cultic behavior and divination, of teaching that slaves were free, of not participating in pagan festivals or even being atheists because they did not bow before the idols of Rome. But the command to serve as lights in darkness shines from the pages of the New Testament all the way back to Jesus' words in the Sermon on the Mount (Matthew 5:14–16) which may have enlightened Peter's mind as he wrote the present passage.

Lights in the darkness—we occupy a privileged position. We would hope the world sees loving wisdom as we participate in the knowing, growing, and showing process of these young people.

Harold Wilke tells the story of his childhood as a little boy with no arms. One day as he struggled to get into a shirt, his mother watched with tears in her eyes. A neighbor, also in the room, said to his mother with some irritation in her voice, "Why don't you help him?"

Wilke's mother responded, "I am helping him."

Growing Christians need all the help they can get, but sometimes that help best comes by allowing us to develop our lives with only the heavenly Father ministering to us through the Holy Spirit. From those precious moments we learn to *know, grow* and *show.*

> Some chisel their fame in blocks of stone,
> Artists paint a canvas screen,
> In songs or rhymes the poets live on
> And on history's pages are seen.

But a faithful teacher outlives them all;
For he carves on the lives of youth,
And helps them answer life's noblest call—
To follow Eternal Truth!

In time's marathon she has no peers,
Through this world her feet do not mire.
Her influence grows with the passing years.
For her students all carry her "fire."

As long as time stands, his work stands too;
He lives, not for art, but for men.
His work is the growing of artists true,
And therefore, his life cannot end.

ENDNOTES

1. Barbara Kantrowitz, "Who Cares About Day Care?" *Newsweek* (28 March 1988): 73.
2. *The Dallas Morning News* (1994).
3. Edwin A. Blum, *Expositor's Bible Commentary, Vol. 12*, ed. Frank E. Gaebelein (Grand Rapids: Zondervan, 1981), 231.

CHAPTER ELEVEN

1988

GO THEREFORE AND TEACH

om en earth.
is in earth.
om 19 Go ye therefore, and teach 20
th all nations, baptizing them in 144
the name of the Father, and of 7
Son, and of the Hō'lў Ghōst

Matthew 28:16-20

During the past two decades student enrollment in church education programs is down 37 percent[1] while other statistics indicate 30 percent of adults may attend Sunday school once a month.[2] Multiple and varied reasons have been offered for this shrinkage, ranging from a lack of commitment to the failure of traditional educational ministries to meet the needs of late twentieth-century people. Probably both reasons and many more have validity, but usually it helps to explore the problem rather than the symptoms. If we attack the figless tree at its roots, we may find the church's neglect of the great teaching commission.

No one can challenge the direct application of this passage to the church and its wider ministry. But in many ways, Christian schools represent a major portion of the mantle of Christian education. To put it another way, Christian education means more than just church education. In our day it has come also to signify education in schools at all levels. The Great Commission has never fallen upon the shoulders of pastors and church staffs alone; it belongs to every believer since we all share the universal priesthood. For teachers, this passage becomes a ringing declaration of duty.

Matthew 28:16–20 offers New Testament readers a commission narrative much like those found in Genesis 12, Exodus 3 and Isaiah 6. Matthew alone records this mountain meeting and has already noted two references to it by the

Lord (*vv.* 26:32; 28:10) and one by the Resurrection angel (*v.* 28:7). Mainline orthodoxy, particularly as evidenced by twentieth-century evangelicals, holds a traditional and somewhat normative interpretation of these five dramatic verses. We seem to believe this paragraph lays the foundation for the modern missionary movement. We gravitate to this text during missionary conferences while failing to see two crucial dimensions of the passage:

1.   These verses mandate both evangelism and teaching with the latter being at least equal to and quite possibly greater in emphasis.

2.   The commission has been given not to apostles alone nor for missionaries only, but to the church. The entire universal body of Christ stands under the requirements of this great teaching commission.

In this chapter we want to explore the text in detail, giving ourselves to the three helpful questions of any serious inductive Bible study: What does it say? What does it mean? What do I do about it? In overview, this great teaching commission offers five central issues.

OPPORTUNITIES FOR TEACHING ARE SET UP BY OBEDIENCE TO GOD

Then the eleven disciples went to Galilee, to the mountain where Jesus had told them to go. (Matthew 28:16)

Matthew tells us that the eleven disciples went to a mountain in Galilee precisely as they had been told by the Resurrection angel and by the Lord. Many New Testament scholars believe this mountain meeting included not only the eleven but more than five hundred other Galilean believers of whom Paul speaks in 1 Corinthians 15:6. If so, the Lord's words in verses 18–20 were delivered not only to the eleven, but also to scores of others who would make up the foundation of the New Testament church.

Finally the disciples are ready to do what Christ tells them without bickering, arguing or delay. Their obedience demonstrated the readiness of these believers to become Christ's teachers. To put it another way, Christian teaching requires an obedient response to Christ's command and that means a heartfelt, uncoerced obedience. This stands in opposition to a grudging, angry response that is only superficial in nature, covering an inwardly rebellious heart.

For years I sought for an illustration to demonstrate this watered-down obedience and I found it in the record of the Spanish-American War. Apparently the United States Congress came up with the idea of renaming captured Spanish warships after American universities and dubbing the collection "the college fleet." Congress itself named the first two ships the "Harvard" and the "Yale." Admiral Dewey, in charge of American naval forces, considered the idea ludicrous. But as a veteran officer he knew how to obey orders. The next ship he captured he renamed the "Massachusetts Institute of Technology" and after that the "Vermont Normal College for Women." As quickly as it had begun, the college fleet was disbanded. Did he do what was asked? Certainly—on the surface he demonstrated impeccable obedience. Did he obey with genuine joy in order to please the one commanding obedience? Hardly.

Christ wants unflinching obedience to the great teaching commission. He wants enthusiastic followership, not disinterested complaining. An interesting theory has emerged in several secular leadership books in recent years: followers create leaders. Unless we work on followership, we cannot work on leadership. That's a very interesting idea. When we bring it over into the realm of teaching, we talk constantly about preparing, retraining and retooling teachers. Yet without recognizing how to improve our followership of Christ, we may be working with only half an equation.

THE YEAR 1988

- ACSI celebrated its tenth anniversary! During the first ten years, ACSI's student enrollment jumped from 185,687 to 454,382, a 245 percent increase.

- Mr. Joe Smith was presented with a generous "love offering" from ACSI member schools in California to help offset medical expenses as a result of cancer and other complications.

REFLECTING ON THE HISTORY OF ACSI

EVEN AMONG CHRIST'S EARLIEST TEACHERS THERE WERE DOUBTERS

When they saw him, they worshiped him; but some doubted. (Matthew 28:17)

We do not find it surprising that they would worship when seeing the risen Lord. The second part of the verse, however, gives us pause. Who were these doubters? What did they really doubt? Were some of the disciples numbered among these doubters, or just some of the larger group of five hundred?

We cannot say what doubts crossed their minds. They may have wondered whether a resurrection really occurred, or whether the person before them was

> "Christian teachers develop confidence and commitment to their ministries when they sense God has called them to what they do."

really Jesus of Nazareth. The word itself indicates a strong feeling of hesitation. They just didn't know what to do next.

Sound familiar? Many times in my teaching career I have not known what to do next. I have wondered whether I could find my meager abilities sufficient for the tasks God repeatedly threw in my path. That's why these chapters consistently come back to the issue of call. Christian teachers develop confidence and commitment to their ministries when they sense God has called them to what they do. And like any other ministry, it must not be compared with how God has called someone else.

During World War II, Winston Churchill addressed the coal miners during times of great crisis. Said he, "For the next score of years your children and your children's children will ask you, 'What have you done to help win the war?' You may say, some served in the troops, some in submarines . . . I dug the coal that fueled the ships."

When I hear about ministries around the world established by those whom I helped prepare, I may say something similar: "I taught the people who went into the uttermost reaches of the world." That sense of recognizing our value as equippers for the future ministry of Christ keeps teachers going through doubts or questions about our sufficiency.

THE ULTIMATE AUTHORITY FOR CHRISTIAN TEACHING RESIDES WITH THE LORD

> *Then Jesus came to them and said, "All authority in heaven and on earth has been given to me."* (Matthew 28:18)

What is this authority of which Jesus speaks? Authority means official control over things (Philippians 2:5–11; Daniel 7:13–14). Jesus explained to the gathered believers at this mountain meeting, "Make no mistake about it; I alone am Lord of the Church." In a few words the Lord clearly establishes His authority, and the word "all" dominates the rest of the passage—*all* authority, *all* nations, *all* things and throughout *all* days.

Disrespect for authority runs rampant in today's society. From sophisticated multimillion-dollar drug rings to "gangsta rap," parents, policemen, politicians, pastors and yes, even pedagogues are held in increasing contempt.

But we don't solve it by forcing military-style adherence through rules in the Christian school. Our students will better learn respect for authority, including the ultimate authority of the Lord, by watching the way we behave under authority. A teacher's response to administrative guidelines will do as much to influence a student on the issue on authority as any set of lessons we can string together in the classroom.

It comes down to attitude. In one of his books, Tony Campolo tells the story of a factory worker who asked his shop steward what it was like to work in this factory. The shop steward answered with a question of his own: "What was it like at your last job?"

"Oh," said the new worker, "it was a miserable job. I didn't like the work and the bosses were unfair to me."

"Unfortunately," responded the shop steward, "you'll find it much the same here."[3]

Campolo communicated a simple, yet profound principle: the attitudes you choose to express are probably the very ones which will be reflected back to you. Yes, administrators and boards and those with power do use it unfairly on occasion. I do not advocate thoughtless submission to demeaning abuse. But every working system or organization must have some way of expressing and expecting response to decisions.

> "Our students will better learn respect for authority, including the ultimate authority of the Lord, by watching the way we behave under authority."

Remember, ultimate authority belongs to the Lord. Our worldly concepts of "born leaders," "rule" and dictatorial behavior in any office of the body betrays our misunderstanding of this verse. Our Lord's words serve to warn papal principals, entrepreneurial elders and bombastic board members that there is only one authority in the church. The only Biblical spirit at the human level must be a mutual yielding and submission.

TEACHING IS CENTRAL IN THE MINISTRY OF CHRIST'S CHURCH

"Therefore go and make disciples of all nations, baptizing them in the name of the Father and of the Son and of the Holy Spirit, and teaching them to obey everything I have commanded you." (Matthew 28:19–20)

The introductory word "therefore" points back to the Lord's authority and forward to the universality of the Gospel and the limitations of the time. New Testament commentators emphasize with one voice that this portion of our passage contains three participles (going, baptizing, teaching) but only one command: "Make disciples."

Center stage in the commission stands that lonely imperative, "Make disciples." How we understand the meaning of that command determines what we do in Christian education. Many have taken it to mean sharing the Gospel and have thereby limited the Great Commission to evangelism at home and abroad. But "disciples," Biblically understood, hear, understand and obey Jesus' teaching. That doesn't happen by raising a hand or coming forward in a meeting. Jesus emphasizes life change, not content transmission. He highlights multiplication of the body in the world, not addition of members on the roll.

> " 'Make disciples.' How we understand the meaning of that command determines what we do in Christian education."

What does discipling mean in the Christian school? Faced with the enormous body of knowledge our students must absorb, harassed by the information explosion whose minefields erupt constantly at our feet, driven by unrelenting lesson plans, we stand ever in danger of over-emphasizing the cognitive domain, of participating in the intellectual idolatry I have mentioned before. To be sure, knowledge forms a part of discipleship and Jesus never extolled ignorance. But discipleship is far more affective and behavioral than cognitive. Somehow in the pressure-packed curriculum which boards, administrators and parents expect us to cover, we must find time to make disciples.

Let's make it as clear as possible. As important as the church's teaching ministry becomes in the light of this passage, Christian parents have no Biblical excuse for surrendering spiritual development of their own children to any other group—church, school, youth organization or camp. Surrogate child care is a subject concerning which I have strong opinions but they are not appropriately offered here. Here we need to understand that many Christian parents, having done all they can to advance the spiritual development of their children at home, now gladly turn to Christian schools to assist, affirm and augment that task. If the evangelical church does not cherish and nourish that teaching ministry, it will miss a great opportunity God has given it in our day.

> "Somehow in the pressure-packed curriculum which boards, administrators and parents expect us to cover, we must find time to make disciples."

CHRIST'S PRESENCE PROVIDES THE KEY TO TEACHING EFFECTIVENESS

"And surely I am with you always, to the very end of the age." (Matthew 28:20)

About whom did Jesus speak these words? About the disciples and the larger mountain multitude? They were surely included, but could hardly qualify for the full term of the promise. The Lord offers His constant presence to His teachers from that day to this.

The traditional word "world," as the King James Version reads, has confused some. I recall even as a college student thinking that the final promise of Matthew's gospel was geographical, i.e., wherever across the globe God might send me, the presence of Christ goes too. Very true, but that's not what this verse says. The Lord promises His presence through the Holy Spirit for every member of the body until the end of the *age.*

> "When the wisdom of the Savior controls truth-teaching, miracles form and monotony fades."

Survival in Christian teaching hinges upon moment by moment dependence on the Holy Spirit during both preparation and presentation. A few days earlier the eleven had heard a promise of great value to teachers:

> But when he, the Spirit of truth, comes, he will guide you into all truth. He will not speak of his own; he will speak only what he hears, and he will tell you what is yet to come. He will bring glory to me by taking from what is mine and making it known to you. All that belongs to the Father is mine. That is why I said the Spirit will take from what is mine and make it known to you. (John 16:13–15)

I refuse to limit the impact of that verse to the recording of the New Testament. For me it represents the presence of the living Lord everywhere His teachers struggle to explain and apply truth. When the wisdom of the Savior controls truth-teaching, miracles form and monotony fades. A neurotic compulsion to duty, characterizing so much Christian teaching, gives way to genuine joy. Any other energizing force, however carefully contrived, offers no more than a substitute.

Countless times in teachers' meetings I have told and retold the wonderful story which appears in the Campolo book I mentioned earlier.

Teddy Stallard was a boy that Miss Thompson just didn't like, and for good reason. He just didn't seem interested in school. There was a dead-pan, blank expression on his face and his eyes had a glassy, unfocused appearance. When she spoke to Teddy, he always answered in monosyllables. His clothes were musty and his hair was unkempt. He wasn't an attractive boy and he certainly wasn't likable.

Whenever she marked Teddy's papers, she got a certain perverse pleasure out of putting X's next to the wrong answers and when she put the F's at the top of the papers, she always did it with a flair. She should have known better; she had Teddy's records and she knew more about him than she wanted to admit. The records read:

First Grade: Teddy shows promise with his work and attitude, but poor home situation.

Second Grade: Teddy could do better. Mother is seriously ill. He receives little help at home.

Third Grade: Teddy is a good boy, but too serious. He is a slow learner. His mother died this year.

Fourth Grade: Teddy is very slow, but well-behaved. His father shows no interest.

Christmas came and the boys and girls in Miss Thompson's class brought her Christmas presents. They piled their presents on her desk and crowded around to watch her open them. Among the presents, there was one from Teddy Stallard. She was surprised that he had brought her a gift, but he had. Teddy's gift was wrapped in brown paper and was held together with Scotch tape. On the paper were written the simple words, "For Miss Thompson from Teddy." When she opened Teddy's present, out fell a gaudy rhinestone bracelet, with half the stones missing, and a bottle of cheap perfume.

The other boys and girls began to giggle and smirk over Teddy's gifts, but Miss Thompson at least had enough sense to silence them by immediately putting on the bracelet and putting some of the perfume on her wrist. Holding her wrist up for the other children to smell, she said,

"Doesn't it smell lovely?" And the children, taking their cue from the teacher, readily agreed with "oo's" and "ah's."

At the end of the day, when school was over and the other children had left. Teddy lingered behind. He slowly came over to her desk and said softly, "Miss Thompson… Miss Thompson, you smell just like my mother… and her bracelet looks real pretty on you too. I'm glad you liked my presents."

When Teddy left, Miss Thompson got down on her knees and asked God to forgive her.

The next day when the children came to school, they were welcomed by a new teacher. Miss Thompson had become a different person. She was no longer just a teacher; she had become an agent of God. She was now a person committed to loving her children and doing things for them that would live on after her. She helped all the children, but especially the slow ones, and especially Teddy Stallard. By the end of that school year, Teddy showed dramatic improvement. He had caught up with most of the students and was even ahead of some.

She didn't hear from Teddy for a long time. Then one day, she received a note that read: "Dear Miss Thompson: I wanted you to be the first to know. I will be graduating second in my class. Love, Teddy Stallard." Four years later, another note came: "Dear Miss Thompson: They just told me I will be graduating first in my class. I wanted you to be the first to know. The university has not been easy, but I liked it. Love, Teddy Stallard." And, four years later: "Dear Miss Thompson: As of today, I am Theodore Stallard, M.D. How about that? I wanted you to be the first to know. I am getting married next month, the 27th to be exact. I want you to come and sit where my mother would sit if she were alive. You are the only family I have now; Dad died last year. Love, Teddy Stallard."

Miss Thompson went to that wedding and sat where Teddy's mother would have sat. She deserved to sit there; she had done something for Teddy that he could never forget.[4]

Teaching! Teachers! God bless us everyone.

ENDNOTES

1. Evangelical Teacher Training Association, *Journal of Adult Training* 2, no. 1 (Fall 1989): 6.
2. George Barna, *The Barna Report, 1992–93* (Ventura, Calif.: Regal, 1992), 126.
3. Tony Campolo, *Who Switched the Price Tags?* (Dallas, Tex.: Word Publishing Co., 1986), 109.
4. Campolo, *Switched*, 69–77.

CHAPTER TWELVE

1989

CHILDREN SHALL BE TAUGHT OF THE LORD

> carbuncles, and all thy
> ...ders of pleasant stones.
> 13 And all thy children *shall* pa...
> *be* taught of the LORD; and 8
> great *shall be* the peace of thy you...
> ...ildren.
> ...hteousness shalt th...

Isaiah 54:9-17

P eace I leave with you; my peace I give you. I do not give to you as the world gives" (John 14:27). Peace . . . what a wonderful word conjuring visions of quiet valleys and calm lakes, children playing happily, adults in harmony with one another, a backdrop of birds raising their voices in song and perhaps a gentle breeze to keep the temperature just right. Special moments like that do come, but most of us do not live with that kind of peace. The fallen world in which we live and work reflects discord and disruption rather than peace and harmony.

Though we in North America stand above many of our international neighbors in affluence and standard of living, we still participate in worldwide problems such as AIDS, the shadow of nuclear holocaust, and the twin social scandals of abuse and abortion. Worldwide some two hundred thousand women die each year as a result of illegal abortions and the chances that a pregnant American woman would choose to have an abortion now stand at one in four.[1]

One would hope the church could present a brighter picture, but Barna reports that across the board people are spending less time participating in church activities.[2] Only 25 percent of all self-proclaimed Christians read the Bible daily.

News from the family front sounds even more frustrating. The divorce rate has doubled since 1965 and one-third of all children born in the 1980s will probably live in a stepfamily before they are eighteen. About 22 percent of children today were born out of wedlock and one out of every five children in America lives in poverty.[3]

In the midst of this alien environment God has called some to be teachers. James Hilton's words in *Goodbye Mr. Chips* were never more true:

> If I had a child who wanted to be a teacher, I would bid him God speed as if he were going to war. For indeed the war against prejudice, greed and ignorance is eternal, and those who dedicate themselves to it give their lives no less because they may live to see some fraction of the battle won.[4]

From Old Testament days to the present hour, teaching has always been a focal point in God's system. In Isaiah 54–57, the prophet speaks of the great salvation which will someday come to Israel on the basis of the grace and work of God's Servant. Unlike Israel, the Messianic servant does *not* fail but establishes the kingdom of peace forever. One of its characteristics appears in Isaiah 54:13: "All your sons will be taught by the Lord, and great will be your children's peace."

In Isaiah's day, in ours, or in the future kingdom, God's teachers draw their effectiveness from this Biblical model. The verses surrounding our chapter title suggest several characteristics of what it means to teach in God's behalf.

GOD WANTS TO GIVE HIS TEACHERS PEACE

"To me this is like the days of Noah, when I swore that the waters of Noah would never again cover the earth. So now I have sworn not to be angry with you, never to rebuke you again. Though the mountains be shaken and the hills be removed, yet my unfailing love for you will not be shaken nor my covenant of peace be removed," says the Lord, who has compassion on you. (Isaiah 54:9–10)

"Do not portray a distant and angry God."

The prophet writes the words of the Lord linking past and future. Bible readers are unaccustomed to finding references to "the days of Noah" (Job 22:16; Matthew 24:38; 1 Peter 3:20; 2 Peter 2:5), but in most cases the phrase appears as a negative warning, evoking images of the worldwide flood. Here God directs our thinking to the post-flood rainbow time when His promises prevail and His punishment has passed.

At that time, we learn, a covenant of peace will prevail because "My unfailing love for you will not be shaken." How does the Christian song of the seventies put it?

> If the highest mountains turn to ashes;
> If the mighty rivers should run dry;
> Should sun and moon grow dim,
> I still will trust in Him.
> He's watching from above;
> I'm resting in His love.[5]

Yes, God wants to give His teachers peace and He wants them to reflect that peace into the lives of children and young people whose existence knows too much trouble and turmoil. What does that actually mean? How do you and I as God's teachers, reflecting the pattern of the Messianic servant, spread peace in the classroom and on the campus?

One way is to make sure we *do not portray a distant and angry God*. Small children especially see in their parents and teachers a picture of God. If life is constantly negative and punitive, they reason, God must be like that. It comes as no surprise to educational leaders that people (including students) have strange ideas about the nature of God.

Second, we reflect the pattern of the Messianic Servant by making sure we *do not squelch the unfailing love* God wants to show others through us. It's one thing to draw upon His grace for our own needs, and that's very important; but we must also be channels of that grace to our students.

We educators make a great deal of the term "alumni." The word comes from the Latin verb *allere* meaning "to nurture." Students who have spent even a semester in our halls are alumni and the school has become their *alma mater* (foster mother). To be sure, we never want a Christian school to stand in any substitute position for parents who can function properly for the inculcation of spiritual and moral values. Nevertheless, for many of our students we do become a genuine *alma mater* because we did show our students parental love.

Third, I remind you (as I remind myself with some regularity), *don't let present struggles detract from future blessings*. Teachers can easily get entangled with some current crisis and lose sight of long-range goals. Yet, of all people, we are trained to plan for and expect outcomes. Our orderly psyches have little taste for confusion.

> "Do not squelch the unfailing love God wants to show others through us."

> "Don't let present struggles detract from future blessings."

A group of professional men having lunch one day argued among themselves about the world's oldest profession. One suggested it must be either farming or ranching since those were occupations followed by Cain and Abel. Another noted God's divine surgery on Adam to create Eve and offered medicine as the oldest profession. Still a third insisted Creation itself was an engineering feat and therefore that profession existed even before Adam and Eve. After a moment a school principal said, "Surely education is the oldest profession because even before Creation the Bible tells us everything was in chaos."

What is the current crisis in your school? Financial survival? An insufficient number of students to make up reasonable grade populations? Hopelessly inadequate facilities? Internal squabbles and hassles among personnel? When our expectations for long-range outcomes seem to corrode, God's peace becomes crucial.

GOD WANTS TO GIVE HIS TEACHERS STRENGTH

O afflicted city, lashed by storms and not comforted, I will build you with stones of turquoise, your foundations with sapphires. I will make your battlements of rubies, your gates of sparkling jewels and all your walls of precious stones. (Isaiah 54:11–12)

The strength of these verses seems to be of two types—material and spiritual. Surely the direct interpretation refers to the rebuilding of Jerusalem and the precious stones probably symbolize God's great love and care.

The traditional application of this metaphor describes the children we teach. In the nineteenth century, William Cushing wrote:

When He cometh, when He cometh to make up His jewels
All His jewels, precious jewels, His loved and His own.
Little children, little children who love their redeemer
Are the jewels, precious jewels, His loved and His own.

Without denying the sentiment, I wonder if a more realistic application might find teachers representing the splendor of that reflection. To be sure, it spiritualizes the text, but I'm quite prepared to say that those who carry out their ministry of Christian teaching symbolize the light of God's glory from which they get their beauty.

Do Christian teachers need material and physical strength? Indeed they do. Buildings and budgets are very much part of the task. Adequate salaries, properly equipped classrooms, reasonable insurance coverage and retirement benefits—these all help create the environment in which we function as professionals. No emotional appeal to sacrificial service can relieve boards from providing the issues of material strength.

But most of us acknowledge that spiritual strength is the real issue in Christian teaching. Isaiah puts it this way.

All your sons will be taught by the Lord, and great will be your children's peace. In righteousness you will be established: Tyranny will be far from you; you will have nothing to fear. Terror will be far removed; it will not come near you. If anyone does attack you, it will not be my doing; whoever attacks you will surrender to you. (Isaiah 54:13–15)

At least four elements surface in this passage as characteristic of spiritual strength. The first is *wisdom*, so much more important than knowledge in Christian teaching. T. S. Eliot once wrote, "All our knowledge only brings us closer to our ignorance, and all our ignorance closer to death. But closer to death, no nearer to God." Christian teachers traffic in knowledge and wisdom. Both must bring their students closer to God, regardless of the title on the door or the subject on the board.

A second item here is *peace*, a theme we have already touched from the passage. When linking peace with spiritual strength, let's remember that the presence or absence of material blessings carries no weight here. Better buildings and budgets do not necessarily indicate greater blessing. God gives peace that goes far beyond immediate circumstance or what may look like blessing or lack of blessing. We move closer to peace when we learn to say, "We're struggling with financial problems. God has blessed us by making us totally dependent on Him."

> "All our knowledge only brings us closer to our ignorance, and all our ignorance closer to death. But closer to death, no nearer to God."
> ~ T. S. Eliot

Remember our focus here—spiritual strength. In the midst of the clamor and confusion of a normal school day, the Word of God still says to all of us, "In quietness and trust is your strength" (Isaiah 30:15).

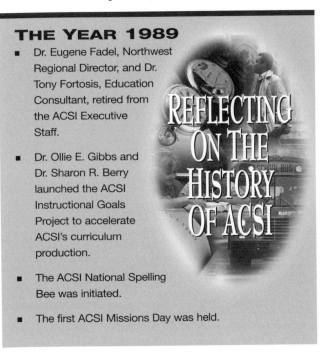

THE YEAR 1989

- Dr. Eugene Fadel, Northwest Regional Director, and Dr. Tony Fortosis, Education Consultant, retired from the ACSI Executive Staff.

- Dr. Ollie E. Gibbs and Dr. Sharon R. Berry launched the ACSI Instructional Goals Project to accelerate ACSI's curriculum production.

- The ACSI National Spelling Bee was initiated.

- The first ACSI Missions Day was held.

REFLECTING ON THE HISTORY OF ACSI

A former colleague tells the story of a nervous teenager at a lakeside baptismal. Just before he was put under he hollered, "I don't want to do this." Putting aside for the moment whether or not he was really baptized in obedience, how often you and I find ourselves with that kind of spirit. How often, therefore, must we find peace, strength and pliability in the disciplines through which the Lord puts us.

Righteousness forms a third focus. Surely the production of righteous behavior in ourselves and our students sustains a certain urgency for all of us. I'm reminded of the college student describing his curriculum: "I started majoring in biology, then I switched to English, and now I'm majoring in geology. It's not much for making a living, but I'm really good at Trivial Pursuit." As much fun as Trivial Pursuit may be, it hardly represents the mission of Christian teaching. We target spiritual, moral and ethical values.

Finally, our passage promises *freedom from fear during attack*. Interesting that the text does not promise freedom *from* attack, something quite different. To be sure Christian schools do not face the moral deterioration of urban public systems. Nevertheless, we must acknowledge dramatic changes in the minds and hearts of our students in recent years.

For example, the *New York Times* reported about fifteen years ago the chief fears of a junior high school student in order of severity: animals, dark rooms, high places, strangers, loud noises. In the most recent *Times* analysis, those five items were changed to: divorce of their parents, nuclear war, lung cancer, pollution, getting mugged.

As teachers, our own fears may also have grown. But God is not limited by any sense of finiteness. For the struggles of their own lives, and to assist their students in the struggles of life, God gives His teachers strength.

GOD GIVES HIS TEACHERS VICTORY

"See, it is I who created the blacksmith who fans the coals into flame and forges a weapon fit for its work. And it is I who have created the destroyer to work havoc; no weapon forged against you will prevail, and you will refute every tongue that accuses you. This is the heritage of the servants of the Lord, and this is their vindication from me," declares the Lord. (Isaiah 54:16–17)

Victory belongs to the people of God because their enemies are in His control. In the context of this passage, He delivers Israel from those who would *create* the implements of attack (the blacksmith) as well as those who would *use* them (the destroyer). Who are these enemies for the Christian teacher? At times, of course, they seem to take the faces of administrators or board members. In other situations, perhaps state or federal officials.

Ultimately, however, I wonder if our greatest enemy is not within—criticism and complaining. To be sure, we work in less than perfect circumstances much of the time, but we must expect that in a war zone. I believe God has called Christian teachers to stand in the gap between fragmented families and a corrupt culture.

> "Apart from a miracle of God's grace, we will *not* turn this society around, but we can make a difference with those kids whose lives we touch everyday."

Apart from a miracle of God's grace, we will *not* turn this society around, but we can make a difference with those kids whose lives we touch everyday. Which reminds us that our passage emphasizes that the victory of Christian teachers remains in God's control No weapon forged against us will prevail. "You will refute every tongue," says the prophet, and you will be vindicated by the Lord. Once again, let's acknowledge that we make only secondary application to our role as the reflectors of the teaching Servant.

What does it take to implement this kind of victory? The old hymn states it well—"Faith is the victory." And remember, Christian faith becomes significant not because of its own quality or strength or amount, but because of its object. Christian teachers need faith in the God who gives them peace, strength and victory.

The African impala can jump to a height of over ten feet and cover a distance of more than thirty feet, yet these magnificent creatures can be kept in an enclosure in any zoo with a three foot wall. How? Impalas will not jump if they cannot see where their feet will fall. Faith in the God who gives His teachers peace and strength and victory is what makes possible the kind of spiritual, moral, ethical and instructional breakthroughs which God will provide for us. We know where our feet will fall—straight into the loving presence of our sovereign Lord.

Notice the way chapter 55 begins. The offer of peace, strength and victory comes *not* to those who have everything together and ride some current wave of success. Note the humble recipients of the Lord's gracious offer:

Come, all you who are thirsty, come to the waters; and you who have no money, come, buy and eat! Come, buy wine and milk without money and without cost. Why spend money on what is not bread, and your labor on what does not satisfy? Listen, listen to me, and eat what is good, and your soul will delight in the richest of fare.

As the rain and the snow come down from heaven, and do not return to it without watering the earth and making it bud and flourish, so that it yields seed for the sower and bread for the eater, so is my word that goes out from my mouth: It will not return to me empty, but will accomplish what I desire and achieve the purpose for which I sent it. (Isaiah 55:1–2; 10–11)

> "And remember, Christian faith becomes significant not because of its own quality or strength or amount, but because of its object."

So I call you my brothers and sisters to a ministry of sacrificial love which enables the teaching servant of Isaiah to reflect and reproduce His light and life in you through the difficult days of this decade. *Sometimes it will require more than you feel you can give.*

In December 1988, Susanna Petrosyan was trapped flat on her back under the rubble of the Armenian earthquake. The lifeless body of her sister-in-law lay next to her and her four-year-old daughter was trapped on the other side. The dehydrated child cried for something to drink, "I thought my child was going to die of thirst," Petrosyan recalled. "I had no water, no fruit juice, no liquids. It was then that I remembered that I had my own blood." The young mother sliced open her index finger with a chard and put it into her daughter's mouth squeezing it so the blood would drain down the child's throat; then another finger, and another, and in that way she sustained the child's life for eight days until they were found.

For us there may be no earthquakes but there are plenty of spiritually dehydrated children whom God has called us to serve. May the words of the new Jerusalem describe your school: "All your sons will be taught by the Lord, and great will be your children's peace."

ENDNOTES

1. Martin E. Marty, "Context: A Commentary on the Interaction of Religion and Culture," *Claretian Publications* 21, no. 8 (15 April 1989): 3.
2. Barna, *What Americans Believe* (Ventura, Calif.: Regal Books, 1991), 68.
3. Barbara Kantrowitz and Pat Wingert, "Step by Step," *Newsweek* (Winter/Spring 1990): 24.
4. James Hilton, *Goodbye Mr. Chips* (Garden City, N.Y.: Doubleday, 1933).
5. Pelle Karlsson, *Unfailing Love* (Irving, Tex.: Word, Inc., 1982).

CHAPTER THIRTEEN

1990

CHILDREN WALKING IN TRUTH

in truth and love.
and 4 I rejoiced greatly that
that found of thy children walking
in truth, as we have received a
commandment from the Father.
And now I beseech thee

2 John

How would you describe the commodity of Christian schools? What precisely do we sell? Since parents and friends give us money so that children and young people may attend our classes, one can assume that some product or service changes hands. Someone may immediately respond by saying, "education." To be sure, we do sell education, but so does every public or private school in America. Surely our accounts receivable list reflects concern for something more than education. Others will emphasize spiritual atmosphere, or perhaps the godly presence of a Christian teacher in every classroom. Some will want to talk about academic excellence, citing test scores and comparative national norms of Christian schools and public schools at some given grade level.

My view ranges somewhat broader than any of the above, as important as they all may be. One could surely argue that the *commodity of the Christian school is truth.* For years I have taught graduate and undergraduate students that no compromise exists between rationalism and revelationism as educational philosophies. Either God has spoken or He has not. Either absolute truth can form the basis of a school curriculum or it cannot. Every Christian school worthy of the name adopts a revelational stance, affirming God's truth as the heart and core of its entire operation. That is what we sell.

Truth—a significant word in any age, to any people, at any time. And a significant word in the Bible, falling often from the lips of our Lord, and appearing frequently in the writings of prophets and apostles. Therefore, one finds it a strange commentary on humanity that this all-important concept can so easily be cast aside in grievous times such as those in which we now live. People sacrifice truth for the sake of peace; people sacrifice truth for the sake of unity; people sacrifice truth for the sake of pleasure. But in the sight of God, truth is final; its determination hardly depends upon our own preferences.

> "The commodity of the Christian school is truth."

Watching his class take a true-false test, a high school teacher noticed a young man flipping a coin before writing each answer. "What are you doing?" he asks the student.

"Taking the test," the young man replies. "Heads is true and tails is false."

The period ends, and as the teacher collects the papers he sees the student frantically flipping the coin and staring at his exam. "And what are you doing now?" asks the teacher.

"Checking my answers."[1]

In many books of the Bible, truth holds a key place. Yet one book seems often overlooked, little quoted, preached even less; but it holds a tremendous impact for us moderns. The epistle of truth—2 John.

The elder, to the chosen lady and her children, whom I love in the truth—and not I only, but also all who know the truth. (2 John 1)

John introduces the epistle in verse 1 and divides the remainder very clearly into two basic units. The first speaks of *truth demonstrated* (*vv.* 2–6), and the second of *truth violated* (*vv.* 7–11). The last two verses form a personal close such as one would find at the end of any first-century letter.

TRUTH DEMONSTRATED

Because of the truth, which lives in us and will be with us forever: Grace, mercy and peace from God the Father and from Jesus Christ, the Father's Son, will be with us in truth and love. It has given me great joy to find some of your children walking in the truth, just as the Father commanded us. And now, dear lady, I am not writing you a new command but one we have had from the beginning. I ask that we love one another. And this is love: that we walk in obedience to his commands. As you have heard from the beginning, his command is that you walk in love. (2 John 2–6)

Lying seems to come easily to all of us. It may begin when young children quickly deny wrongdoing in order to keep from being punished. As adults we sometimes avoid telling the whole truth in order to advance our own causes or perhaps to save money. In 2 John 1–6, John takes immediate aim at the importance of truth, reminding us that Jesus came to earth in truth and love.

Whether "the chosen lady" (*v.* 1) represents a local church or a real person, the central theme of this tiny epistle stands firm—truth. After a loving introduction, the apostle suggests three ways in which God's truth is demonstrated.

Truth Is Established through the Father's Word

The Father's truth has been shown firsthand through His Son who revealed grace, mercy, and peace— qualities marking not only the life of our Lord, but also the lives of those who follow Him.

All the elements of salvation emanating from God were visible in that church and, by God's grace, have been demonstrated in the lives of every Christian from the days of John until now. God reached out and utilized this opportunity to demonstrate Himself to an assembly of people—His grace, His mercy, His peace, His truth and His love. All this came from the triune Godhead as gifts to believers.

Let's return again to my earlier remarks about rationalism and revelationism. Since the role of the Bible in Christian schools represents a formative and normative guideline, every course and behavior falls under its plumb line evaluation. That doesn't deny the use of reason nor does it argue

THE YEAR 1990

- The combined student enrollment in ACSI member schools exceeded a half-million students for the first time. The actual figure was 503,172.

- Dr. Phil Renicks, Dr. Art Nazigian and Mr. Henry Toews were the first ACSI team to go behind the fallen Iron Curtain to Romania to help start the first Christian school in a former Communist country.

- The first ACSI field office was established outside of the United States. The Latin America office was established in Guatemala City.

- The ACSI Preschool Accreditation Program was introduced.

- Mrs. Eunice Dirks retired after eighteen years of faithful service to ACSI.

REFLECTING ON THE HISTORY OF ACSI

that Christians shouldn't be rational. It does emphasize where our schools find their truth source. Notice this helpful paragraph from Alister McGrath:

> Classical Christian theology, including all responsible evangelical theology, makes use of reason—for example, in thinking through the implications of certain aspects of God's self-revelation. For example, consider the role of reason in exploring the relation between a functional and ontological Christology: if Jesus is our Savior, yet only God can save, reason suggests that Jesus must (in some sense of the word) be God. Yet here reason is reflecting on revelation, seeking to explore its implications. Rationalism declares that all thinking about God must be based upon human reason, thus immediately locking theology into the fallen human situation, with no possibility of being extricated from our confusion and distortion by God himself.[2]

We want so much from our students in godly behavior patterns. It may be worthwhile to remember that absolute morality is absolutely linked to absolute truth. The assumption that truth has no absolute base seriously affects teenagers making life decisions.

Each year more than a million American teens become pregnant, four out of five of them unmarried, thirty thousand of them under age fifteen. If present trends continue, 40 percent of today's fourteen-year-old girls will be pregnant at least once before the age of twenty.[3] While the young women face the consequences, we don't want to let the young men off the hook. Without external standards which they may confidently cite, they may not find adequate inner strength to fight their hormonal rages or peer pressures. All of which leads us directly to a second demonstration of truth.

Truth Is Demonstrated through "Some of Your Children"

Is John referring to a remnant of the congregation or the young people of the church? Commentators vary in their views, but one thing seems clear, the Bible commends all who live out their faith by walking in the truth.

But we find ourselves almost startled by the word "some." Obviously since *some* were walking in the truth, *others* were not. Some error of doctrine, perhaps a cult of false knowledge, had pierced this Christian community and turned hearts away from God.

That reality marks our own day as well. Of almost any Christian congregation (or Christian school), one could say that some walk seemingly blameless lives of integrity following God's command directly whereas others falter along the way. Within the context of Johannine writings, the reference to the "command" in both verses 4 and 5 takes us back to 1 John 3:23: "And this is his command: to believe in the name of his Son, Jesus Christ, and to love one another as he commanded us."

To walk in truth does not mean merely to believe the truth. To walk in truth does not even refer only to a particular time in which one's life was changed by the truth. Both of these are prerequisite, but walking in truth involves considerably more; it denotes continual conduct and behavior in the realm of the truth.

Part of the problem with walking in truth on our campuses is that unaccountable lifestyles make it too easy to walk in error. How would many Christians react if godly living were regulated like a hockey game? Jacques Plante, a goalie for a professional hockey team, had just come off the ice after a particularly poor performance and responded to a badgering reporter with the following remark: "How would you like a job where, if you make a mistake, a big red light goes on and eighteen thousand people boo?"

In many ways, this goalie found himself accountable to eighteen thousand fans. Most of us do not need quite that many accountability partners, but we all surely need some one or ones with whom we can express ourselves with total honesty and who will hold us to the standards of truth.

As I have frequently asserted in this book, those who work in Christian academia may find one error particularly easy to fall into: the idea that knowledge alone moves one along the sanctification process and in and of itself forms an adequate goal for educators to pursue. We do work in the cognitive domain, but because we teach truth, we expect it to have results in the affective and conative domains as well. Our next point expands on this important idea.

Truth Is Demonstrated through the Love of the Saints

What is more important in a group of believers—truth or love? John argues that these two absolutely essential ingredients must be kept in balance. Just as

Jesus came "full of grace and truth" (John 1:14), He expects His teachers to speak the truth in love, never compromising one for the sake of the other.

According to a legend, the apostle John, more than one hundred years old, preached, "Little children, love one another." Then he repeated himself twice more. Finally, he concluded, "It is enough. Little children, love one another."

But let's not get confused here. The demonstration of love is not shown by the fact that the commandment exists. We show love by obedience to the commandment. When Christians walk in love toward one another, they obey the command of God and that obedience demonstrates their commitment to truth. John Mitchell, retired pastor of Bethany Bible Church in Phoenix, argues that, "Love is sincerely wishing the other person God's very best and taking whatever action is necessary to see that accomplished."

What a wonderful guideline for teachers in a Christian school. Why not put it in your public relations material? "At our school, every teacher sincerely wishes each student God's very best and takes whatever action is necessary to see that accomplished." There is no substitute for this kind of love in any church or Christian school. Talking will not get the job done. We dare not be like the car owner whose mechanic reported, "I couldn't repair your brakes—so I made your horn louder."

Of significant concern on the present horizon are the struggles so many schools experience utilizing church facilities. Linked closely is the attitude of pastors toward Christian education. Somehow the attitude and behavior of this first-century congregation needs to settle in on those struggles so that congregations and Christian school staffs who use shared facilities will still show the world a demonstration of God's truth through the love of the saints for one another.

> A Christian School Motto: "At our school, every teacher sincerely wishes each student God's very best and takes whatever action is necessary to see that accomplished."

TRUTH VIOLATED

Many deceivers, who do not acknowledge Jesus Christ as coming in the flesh, have gone out into the world. Any such person is the deceiver and the antichrist. Watch out that you do not lose what you have worked for, but that you may be rewarded fully. Anyone who runs ahead and does not continue in the teaching of Christ does not have God; whoever continues in the teaching has both the Father and the Son. If anyone comes to you and does not bring this teaching, do not take him into your house or welcome him. Anyone who welcomes him shares in his wicked work. (2 John 7–11)

Perhaps we need to backtrack for a moment here and talk about the theological climate in which John wrote these words. A brief but helpful paragraph describing the occasion and purpose of this epistle appears in *The NIV Study Bible.*

> During the first two centuries the gospel was taken from place to place by traveling evangelists and teachers. Believers customarily took these missionaries into their homes and gave them provisions for their journey when they left. Since Gnostic teachers also relied on this practice, 2 John was written to urge discernment in supporting traveling teachers; otherwise, someone might unintentionally contribute to the propagation of heresy rather than truth.

Interesting. Two thousand years ago, John urged discernment in the choice of teachers. Someone once asks Harry Ironside why there were so many crazies in the body of Christ. Ironside replied, "Wherever there is light there are bugs." This section of our epistle describes false teaching, something against which every Christian school must protect itself continuously.

Americans are a religious lot, but that hardly makes them Biblical Christians. According to the 1991 issue of *American Demographics*, 86.5 percent of American adults claim to be Christian while at the same time 25 percent believe in ghosts and one in six think they have communicated with the dead!

Description of the Deceivers

We have already noted the importance of combining truth and love in our attitudes and behavior. Next, in 2 John 7–13, John emphasized that some people care for neither. These "deceivers" have abandoned the teaching about the Father and the Son; they go beyond the limits of pure doctrine and deliberately confuse and lead astray those who listen to them.

The basic issue is denial of the Incarnation; false teachers do not believe that God came in the flesh in the person of Jesus Christ. Such a person, argues verse 9, denies not only Jesus but has rejected both the Father and the Son. But what should we do with the word "antichrist" at the end of verse 7? It helps to go back to 1 John 2:18 where we read that in addition to one final antichrist, "even now many antichrists have come." Apparently John felt quite free in using that strong terminology to describe teachers wandering from the truth.

Truth violated by pedagogical deception. From the deceivers in this first-century community to David Koresh and cultic religions of the 1990s—how convoluted the world seems in its understanding of truth. One is reminded of James Russell Lowell's striking verse from "The Present Crisis."

> Truth forever on the scaffold.
> Wrong forever on the throne—
> Yet that scaffold sways the future,
> And, behind the dim unknown,
> Standeth God within the shadow,
> Keeping watch above His own.

Reaction to the Deceivers

Watch out that you do not lose what you have worked for, but that you may be rewarded fully. If anyone comes to you and does not bring this teaching, do not take him into your house or welcome him. Anyone who welcomes him shares in his wicked work. (2 John 8, 10, 11)

How should sincere Christians react to such false teachers? John issued two practical warnings: watch out so you don't lose your full reward and don't welcome such people or assist them in any way. Apparently, John's immediate correspondents were already doing this, since he chose wording that suggested they should stop their behavior. The warnings are clear.

> *Do not let down your guard.* (*v.* 8)
> *Do not welcome heretics.* (*v.* 10)
> *Do not share in their wicked work.* (*v.* 11)

We do not have the option of letting down our guard even momentarily because the cultic error of our day is obtuse and insidious. Recently I sent a group of seminary students to the library to compile a list of ten Christian magazines for which they might want to write articles. Upon the receipt of the lists in the next class period, I discovered that two of the twelve had listed a notoriously cultic magazine. When I confronted them only half-jokingly, they both remarked that the articles they scanned in the current issue seemed "okay." That's the problem with heresy; it so often seems okay.

Christian school teachers and students alike must learn to handle heresy the way Dr. Seuss advises:

> My uncle ordered popovers from the restaurant's bill of fare.
> And, when they were served, he regarded them with a penetrating stare.
> Then he spoke great Words of Wisdom as he sat there on that chair:
> "To eat these things," said my uncle, "You must exercise great care.
> You may swallow down what's solid, BUT . . . you must spit out the air!"

And as you partake of the world's bill of fare, that's darned good advice to
  follow.
Do a lot of spitting out the hot air.
And be careful what you swallow.[4]

Like many of us, John felt that touchy matters of doctrine were best dealt
with in person, so he deferred further discussion until he could see his friends.
And at that visit he wanted to accomplish more than just theological correction;
he wanted them all to experience real joy from their collective fellowship. What
a grand picture of the body of Christ—demonstrating truth, avoiding violators
of truth and sharing loving joy with one another.

*I have much to write to you, but I do not want to use paper and ink. Instead, I
hope to visit you and talk with you face to face, so that our joy may be complete.
The children of your chosen sister send their greetings.* (2 John 12–13)

This brief epistle reminds us of the joy of teaching and warns us against
teaching error. The final verse (*v.* 13) refers to another congregation sending a
greeting to the one John addressed here. These paragraphs make it very plain
that when error-ridden religion of human fabrication crumbles into
nothingness, the saints will be singing the redemption song before the Lamb
who Himself is the truth. How glorious that second verse which reminds us that
the truth "lives in us and will be with us forever."

I close with the words of Carl Henry from his stimulating book *Twilight of a
Great Civilization.*

No teacher does serious learning any service who implies the finality of
contemporary culture and represents its conceptual content as the acme of
truth and the criterion of wisdom. Modern culture is the expression of one
particular epoch in the much longer chain of human history, and it has no
authentic basis for claiming ultimacy for its representations of reality, truth
and good.[5]

ENDNOTES

1. James Hassett, *Psychology Today.*
2. Alister McGrath, *Intellectuals Don't Need God & Other Modern Myths* (Grand Rapids: Zondervan, 1992), 147.
3. Claudia Wallis, "The Tragic Costs of Teenage Pregnancy," *Reader's Digest* (April 1986): 99.
4. Theodore Seuss Geisel, "Points to Ponder," *Reader's Digest* (February 1993): 117.
5. Carl F. H. Henry, *Twilight of a Great Civilization* (Westchester, Ill.: Crossway Books, 1988), 92.

CHAPTER FOURTEEN

A HEART TO KNOW ME

up.
.19. 7 And I will give them a h
heart to know me, that I am 7
19. the LORD: and they shall be un
people, and I will be their
they shall return
plant them, and not pluck

Jeremiah 24:1-7

Someone has said Christians believe that the heart of education is education for the heart. The highest achievements in academic testing and athletic awards provide no substitute for the spiritual development of students in Christian schools. That theme can be found in Jeremiah 24.

The historical context sets the passage in 597 B.C., at the beginning of Zedekiah's reign. Jehoiachin and other leaders of Jerusalem have been carried into exile by the Babylonians (2 Kings 24:8–16). Through a parable of good and bad figs, Jehovah tells Jeremiah that the exiles will be restored while those remaining in the land would be destroyed. Nebuchadnezzar needed skilled artisans and construction workers to build the splendors of Babylon. The exiles were shocked into repentance and committed themselves to the single-minded worship of God.

Meanwhile, those who escaped Nebuchadnezzar's fury would now feel the full weight of God's wrath because of their hopeless degradation. Jeremiah likens the good figs (exiles) to the firstfruits offered to God; the bad figs are useless and must be thrown out. In this graphic vision, the prophet demonstrates that fellowship with God and the blessings which come from His grace have no connection with cultic forms, geography, political connection or educational status. It is a matter of the heart.

After Jehoiachin son of Jehoiakim king of Judah and the officials, the craftsmen and the artisans of Judah were carried into exile from Jerusalem to Babylon by Nebuchadnezzar king of Babylon, the Lord showed me two baskets of figs placed in front of the temple of the Lord. One basket had very good figs, like those that ripen early; the other basket had very poor figs, so bad they could not be eaten.

Then the Lord asked me, "What do you see, Jeremiah?"

"Figs," I answered. "The good ones are very good, but the poor ones are so bad they cannot be eaten."

Then the word of the Lord came to me: "This is what the Lord, the God of Israel, says: 'Like these good figs, I regard as good the exiles from Judah, whom I sent away from this place to the land of the Babylonians. My eyes will watch over them for their good, and I will bring them back to this land. I will build them up and not tear them down; I will plant them and not uproot them. I will give them a heart to know me, that I am the Lord. They will be my people, and I will be their God, for they will return to me with all their heart.' " (Jeremiah 24:1–7)

Though you may not agree with the analogy, I want to assume in this chapter that our students are good figs and that our care for them should approximate, on a human level, the Lord's care for the exiles in Babylon. The passage suggests four different dimensions of that care: preservation, restoration, edification and dedication.

MY EYES WILL WATCH OVER THEM
Preservation

It requires little imagination to think of the teaching role as one of preservation. Yes, we want to be innovators, throwing out the baggage of the past in order to make room for new ideas and concepts. But for Christians committed to absolute truth, the heritage of the faith holds enormous importance. Christian schools protect and carry forward that heritage.

Consider, for example, the *preservation of parental authority*. During this century, public education has all but jettisoned any significant parental voice. Christian schools, on the other hand, have loudly proclaimed the importance of parental voice in our educational programs. Yet on a practical level, we sometimes wonder whether some parents don't want a stronger voice than they ought to have or than we would like them to have.

Whatever that might mean administratively, with respect to PTF, policy manuals and the like, I'm concerned that the teacher's eyes watch over Christian school students with a view toward preserving their submission to parental authority. Except in cases of child abuse, we dare not allow ourselves the opportunity for conflict with an authority God has clearly placed higher than our own in the lives of our students.

Interestingly, William James McGuffey, whose name you will instantly recognize, had this concept exactly right back on the Ohio frontier. He once wrote to the superintendents in his jurisdiction:

> Teachers ought to know best *how* to do that which is required of them. Parents are, or ought to be, the better judges of *what is to be done*. . . . But, much as we love, and ought to love those committed to our care, they are but our pupils, not our children. . . . None but the *natural* parent can feel that natural affection which is adequate to the duties of *properly educating* an immortal mind [emphases his].[1]

God also holds Christian school teachers responsible for the *preservation of a spiritual heritage.* In most cases, we are not the ones He uses to lead our students to Christ. Like the apostle Paul working with young Timothy, we perpetuate and protect a spiritual heritage begun by parents and grandparents. Quite frankly, a significant percentage of parents who send their children to our schools anticipate high success on this point and when they fail to see it, their interest quickly wanes.

Consider an illustration from the Catholic parochial system. In 1963, over two hundred Catholic high school seminaries dotted the nation. Now only ten remain. In May 1991, St. Vincent's in Chicago closed after graduating five seniors, only one of whom even considered the priesthood. If we preserve and advance an academic and intellectual climate at the expense and sacrifice of our spiritual heritage, we will have failed our constituents and our Christ.

The eyes of an effective Christian school teacher also watch over the *preservation of educational progress.* We are all links in a chain, members of a team. I talked recently with a sixth grade teacher in a Christian school who struggled to go into her class each morning. Apparently she had inherited

THE YEAR 1991

- President George Bush addressed the ACSI Anaheim convention live via satellite hookup with the White House.

- The ACSI Spelling Series was introduced. This was the first of the many ACSI curriculum projects.

- ACSI joined with Walk Thru The Bible and Campus Crusade for Christ to form "The CoMission."

- The Lifestyles of Christian Teenagers Symposium was sponsored by ACSI in Orlando, Florida.

- The Foreign Exchange Administrators Internship program was established.

REFLECTING ON THE HISTORY OF ACSI

a group of students allowed to run wild by their fifth grade teacher the year before. Assuming an accurate assessment, that fifth grade teacher had failed to preserve educational progress.

Here we have a potential conflict with the preservation of parental authority. The ideal scene pictures teachers clasping each other's hands along with the hands of parents. Often, however, we find ourselves somewhat isolated, depending only upon each other for encouragement and assistance in advancing our students' educational progress. In the 1960s an average parent spent around thirty hours a week with a child, now it is seventeen. Split-shift parenting is a reality among two-income families and only one of six couples today have work schedules that don't overlap.[2]

As does the Lord, the Christian school teacher develops eyes that watch over students with a goal toward preserving parental authority, spiritual heritage and educational progress.

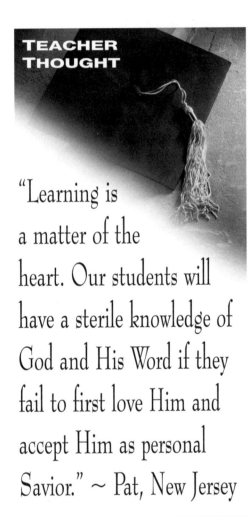

I WILL BRING THEM BACK TO THIS LAND
Restoration

Sometimes we cannot preserve good things in the lives of students. Sometimes those qualities have already fled and the Christian teacher becomes a restorer of what used to be. For example, twenty-seven million Americans are functionally illiterate—that's about one adult in five. Forty-seven million more read only on the most minimal level. Together that represents one-third of our entire adult population.[3]

But we are more likely to face a restoration of less obvious dimensions. For example, a *restoration of self-dignity* in some of our students. Child abuse statistics in America change almost weekly, but all appall a decent mind. One recent report gives these numbers:

One in six adults across American were physically abused in childhood. Almost as many, one is seven, confess that they were victims of sexual abuse as children. Four in ten Americans know someone who was abused as a child. And bear in mind that most of the people abused as children tell no one.[4]

When one puts the best possible framework on available statistics, we are a nation of people harming our own children. Some of those deeply damaged children end up in Christian schools quite confident they have no value and are worthless in the eyes of all adults.

There may have been a day when we could think of those kinds of children as "outside" our world, but we surely now know the untruth of that thought. We do serve a much more privileged clientele than most public schools, but our percentage of problem students and students who have already lost self-dignity increases every year.

I think Christian school teachers should bear some responsibility for *restoring self-discipline*. Not just restoring discipline, but restoring, or if need be creating, a sense of *self*-discipline. I've always viewed Christian school teaching as a discipling process, and no one person becomes a disciple without personal self-discipline. Of course, some of our students come from undisciplined homes. Recently I saw a list of excuses actually written by parents to school authorities.

"My son is under the doctor's care and should not take Physical Education today—please execute him."

"Please excuse my son's tardiness. I forgot to wake him up and I did not find him until I started making the beds."

"Sally won't be in school a week from Friday; we have to attend a funeral."

> "Christian school teachers should bear some responsibility for *restoring self-discipline*. Not just restoring discipline, but restoring, or if need be creating, a sense of *self*-discipline."

> "Producing responsible children from irresponsible parents forms an essential part of our daily task."

Producing responsible children from irresponsible parents forms an essential part of our daily task.

Christian schools also call upon teachers to *restore a sense of self-direction*. We see this at the seminary level as well. In any entering class we can expect about 25 percent who have achieved an acceptable level of maturity; 55 percent who are essentially immature, people in process who struggle with discipline in human relationships and many other problems of life; and about 20 percent bogged down with serious spiritual and emotional problems. Some are educationally deprived; others are Biblically illiterate; many are spiritually naive; and an increasing number are theologically deficient.

We have also discovered an interesting phenomenon. The new "Stranger of the Trinity" is God the Father, a deficiency due in part, perhaps, to the loss of a hymnodic heritage. In the contemporary church, many of our students commonly sing hymns to pronouns rather than members of a personal Godhead.

It's too soon to tell how much of this need for restoration can be blamed on the high tech nature of education today. Many students at all levels seem more comfortable with computers than people. One is reminded of the doctor who called his patient and said, "Diagnostic computers don't make mistakes, Mr. Palmroy; you have Dutch elm disease."

> "There is no secular activity for a Christian."

Just one more thought on the matter of self-direction. I think Christian education at all levels ought to foster a strong sense of vocation in the hearts of its students. In some cases that may mean encouraging high school students to consider Christian college, Bible college, and even seminary. It may mean affirming thoughts about ministry in foreign mission service. At the very least it means a clear-cut understanding that there is no secular activity for a Christian. God's people do what they do because they understand He has called them to it, even when those tasks may be something other than what we had hoped. How did C. T. Studd put it?

> Some wish to live within the sound
> Of church or chapel bell;
> I want to run a rescue shop
> Within a yard of hell.

I WILL BUILD THEM UP AND NOT TEAR THEM DOWN
Edification

In 1990, a commission of educational, political, medical and business leaders met to examine the problems of American children. They issued a report called *Code Blue* which arrived at an unprecedented conclusion: "Never before has one generation of American teenagers been less healthy, less cared for, or less prepared for life than their parents were at the same age." You know the numbers—suicide is now the second leading cause of death among adolescents, having increased 300 percent since 1950; teen pregnancy has risen 621 percent since 1940; the teen homicide rate has increased 230 percent since 1950; and homicide is now the leading cause of death among fifteen- to nineteen-year-old minority youth.

Essentially the *Code Blue* report developed a very interesting premise. It suggests that the challenges to American children and youth are *not* essentially rooted in illness or economics. Rather, the most basic cause of suffering is profoundly self-destructive behavior—drinking, drugs, violence, promiscuity—a crisis of behavior, belief and character.[5]

In this miasmic ocean Christian schools represent islands, safe harbors of repose. Edification, of course, means to build up rather than tear down and Christian school teachers should provide *edification in spiritual formation.* Spiritual formation is not just a matter of knowing Bible stories and memorizing Bible verses, as valuable as both of those may be. *Spiritual formation is much more affective than cognitive, much more related to attitudinal values than assimilated facts.*

According to an NBC news report dated May 4, 1990, five West Point cadets graduated that spring despite being caught cheating on a final examination. The examination was given in a course entitled "Military Ethics." I think Jeremiah would cry a stern warning to any Christian school graduating intellectual giants whose test scores merely hide the fact that they are spiritual pygmies.

> "Spiritual formation is not just a matter of knowing Bible stories and memorizing Bible verses, as valuable as both of those may be. Spiritual formation is much more affective than cognitive, much more related to attitudinal values than assimilated facts."

Does your school, do you in your classroom, recognize the importance of the world beyond the intellectual? Many private schools provide academic excellence. A distinctively Christian school and classroom goes beyond the merely academic to encourage spiritual depth as well.

Donald Whitney identifies spiritual disciplines as one of three ways that growth takes place in our lives (the other two being other people to sharpen us—Proverbs 27:17—and circumstances to stimulate us—Romans 8:28). According to Whitney, these disciplines include, but are certainly not limited to, "Bible intake, prayer, worship, evangelism, service, stewardship, fasting, silence and solitude, journaling, and learning." Notice the relative place of learning on his list. As educators, we cannot place it that low, but it behooves us to give a proper place, and not just lip service, to the others as well.

We must also take responsibility for *edification in social awareness.* This represents third-level integration. The first level is the integration of God's Word with whatever subject matter you teach; the second, the integration of your theologized classes with the other aspects of the curriculum throughout the institution; the third asks whether the student can take the first two levels and make them work in the halls, on the football field and out on the street.

The socially aware Christian school student understands her values, her standards and what it means to be a member of a genuine minority group in an alien culture. He doesn't expect a society which keeps its teachers in poverty while making its professional athletes instant millionaires to have any grasp of eternal values. She rejects the "rights mentality" of American populism in favor of the "responsibility mentality" of the New Testament.

The Christian school teacher also provides *edification in emotional stability.* Children who come to school from homes controlled by screaming parents don't need screaming coaches at basketball practice or frustrated teachers meting out uncalled-for punishments. Your modeling behavior consists not only of quickly solving an equation on a chalkboard or demonstrating effectiveness in public prayer. Nor do you have a choice of whether or not to model. Your behavior stands under the searchlight at all points and the way you handle crisis, abuse, grief, insults, criticism and all the other problems endemic to a teacher's life creates the level to which you can build up emotional stability in your children and young people.

Christian thinker Thomas Merton once wrote, "Every man becomes the image of what he adores. He whose worship is directed to a dead thing becomes a dead thing. He who loves corruption rots. He who loves a shadow becomes himself a shadow."

I WILL GIVE THEM A HEART TO KNOW ME
Dedication

We come to the heart of the passage. Everybody knows teachers are dedicated; there would be no other reason to continue in the profession. In the fall of 1991, the state of Ohio ranked twenty-two out of fifty in average teacher salary with a figure of $30,567. The average teacher salary in the nation that fall was $29,773 and the average state spends $4,606 to educate each student. Meanwhile, beach volleyball players in Fort Myers, Florida, make upwards of $100,000 a year.

Christian teachers must first of all show *dedication to God Himself* and the ability to reproduce that dedication in their students. Once a famous television commentator interviewed Mother Teresa in Calcutta. During the course of the interview he said, "I wouldn't do what you are doing for all the money in the world." Mother Teresa answered, "Neither would I."

Finally, there is a *dedication to serving others*. We are told that social workers and medical personnel are a part of the "helping professions." I dare say there may be no profession more *helping* than that of teaching. If you effectively serve your students through the process of preservation, restoration, edification and dedication, you will help produce a generation of people who not only survive a pagan culture, but who can actually serve God and others in that kind of alien context.

> "Christian teachers must first of all show dedication to God Himself and the ability to reproduce that dedication in their students."

God holds us responsible for these kinds of outcomes, not just for balancing the budget or winning the soccer league.

The last three verses of Jeremiah 24 talk about the bad figs. The reference is, of course, to Zedekiah and the survivors and God's judgment upon them. Yes, there are bad figs in our classes but that is not the focus of this chapter any more than it was the focus of Jeremiah's chapter. God has given our schools thousands of good figs placed in our vineyards for care and nurture. Regarding these children and young people, God says to us, "Give them a heart to know Me."

ENDNOTES

1. John H. Westerhoff III, *McGuffey and His Readers* (Nashville: Abingdon, 1978), 181–182.
2. *Executive Monthly* (September 1991).
3. "Ad Council Coalition for Literacy," *Reader's Digest* (September 1986).
4. James Patterson and Peter Kim, *The Day America Told the Truth* (New York: Prentice Hall, 1991), 125.
5. Dan Coats, "America's Youth: A Crisis of Character," *Imprimis* (September 1991).
6. Donald S. Whitney, *Spiritual Disciplines for the Christian Life* (Colorado Spring: NavPress, 1991), 15–16.

CHAPTER FIFTEEN

1992

TEACHING IN ALL WISDOM

in you, the hope of glory
28 Whom we preach, warning
every man, and teaching every
man in all wisdom; that we to
may present every man perfect
Christ Jē'sus:

rs.

Colossians 1:28-29

What do Christian teachers pray for? Surely to be used by God in their classrooms and, I would think, for a strong measure of energy and physical stamina. In accordance with repeated New Testament injunctions, we pray for wisdom and spiritual power to achieve God's purposes through us.

Amazingly, all these ideas come together in two short verses at the end of the first chapter of Paul's letter to the church at Colosse. While writing these words, Paul languished under house arrest so he speaks with genuine feeling about pain and afflictions (*v.* 24). The verses which make up our Scriptural focus follow a brilliant paragraph on the preeminence or supremacy of Christ (*vv.* 15–23), a passage in which Paul describes his own ministry for the church. He expresses devotion to the great mystery "which is Christ in you, the hope of glory" (*vv.* 24–27). In these paragraphs, we center on Christian teaching—what we do, how we do it, and why we do it.

We proclaim him, admonishing and teaching everyone with all wisdom, so that we may present everyone perfect in Christ. To this end I labor, struggling with all his energy, which so powerfully works in me. (Colossians 1:28–29)

OUR PROCLAMATION

The first three words of verse 28 appear in different syntax in the Greek text, putting the Savior first—"Him we proclaim." The word "proclaim" describes a public announcement and appears only in Acts and the writings of Paul. It carries a distinctive mission message of calling one's hearers directly to the Savior and reminds us that Christian teachers should focus on Christ not a system of rules or even doctrine. To be sure, doctrine is extremely important, but in Christian education, the centrality of a personal walk with the Savior must transcend orderly assimilation of the faith and even developing traits of Biblical behavior.

Paul carries out this proclamation as a servant of the church. I'm fascinated with the wording in verses 24 and 25 where he writes,

> *Now I rejoice in what was suffered for you, and I fill up in my flesh what is still lacking in regard to Christ's afflictions, for the sake of his body, which is the church. I have become its servant by the commission God gave me to present to you the word of God in its fullness.* (Colossians 1:24–25)

Notice the way the great apostle describes himself—as a servant. Although our word "deacon" is a cognate of the original Greek word, in the New Testament the word carries no intent of authority or power, only service. Picking up on the word "servant" we again see that *Christian teaching is a vocation and not a job.* In verse 25 Paul tells us, "I have become its servant by the commission God gave me." The Christian teacher is a commissioned officer in the kingdom, an officer whose entire task is to serve others by proclaiming Christ.

OUR PROCESS

Four words appear in verses 28 and 29 which very specifically depict the process of Christian service and nurture. Each takes the present tense (three are participles and one an active indicative) indicating that *Christian teachers engage in these activities all the time.* First comes ADMONISHING, a word which appears also in 1 Corinthians 10:11, Ephesian 6:4, 1 Corinthians 4:4, and Titus 3:10 and describes the process of setting someone's mind into proper order. What better expression to describe what goes on in our classrooms! We commonly think of admonishment as referring to scolding or warning, but the idea of correcting skewed thinking fits the teaching task even better.

The second word describing our process of instruction is TEACHING itself. We all know well another familiar text in which the words admonishing and teaching appear together, a three-verse paragraph which contains some of the most beautiful phraseology in the New Testament.

> *Let the peace of Christ rule in your hearts, since as members of one body you were called to peace. And be thankful. Let the word of Christ dwell in you richly as you teach and admonish one another with all wisdom, and as you sing psalms, hymns and spiritual songs with gratitude in your hearts to God. And whatever you do, whether in word or deed, do it all in the name of the Lord Jesus, giving thanks to God the Father through him.* (Colossians 3:15–17)

> " 'Teaching' is the orderly presentation of Christian truth for converts so that they may know how to grow." ~ Rick Melick

Dozens of teaching definitions attempt to explain what we do. In his commentary on this passage, my friend and former colleague Dr. Rick Melick offers the simplest and most helpful description I have seen: " 'Teaching' is the orderly presentation of Christian truth for converts so that they may know how to grow." Note the emphasis on order and the observation that Christian teachers handle more than just Biblical information. "Christian truth" covers a wide realm of ministry in churches and Christian schools.

The third word of this quadrant, LABOR, appears in the first part of Colossians 1:29. To achieve the central objective of Christian teaching (which we shall explore in a moment), Paul brings up work. I once heard Peter Drucker say, "Sooner or later everything degenerates into work." How tempting to look at a passage like this and think in lofty, almost mystical terms about what we do. But every experienced teacher knows well the hours of drudgery essential to get the job done and achieve the goals of education.

Notice the switch from "we" to "I" in verse 29. Anyone can give nodding agreement and an occasional "amen" to the overall banner of Christian teaching. But the endless agonizing hours of labor represent a much more personal part of the task. Of this word Peter T. O'Brien writes,

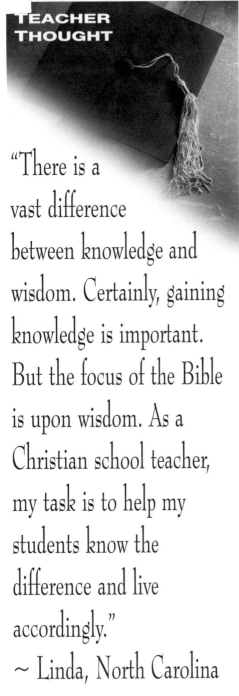

"There is a vast difference between knowledge and wisdom. Certainly, gaining knowledge is important. But the focus of the Bible is upon wisdom. As a Christian school teacher, my task is to help my students know the difference and live accordingly."

~ Linda, North Carolina

Kopiō is a word used in secular Greek of "a beating," "weariness" (as though one had been beaten) and "exertion," the proper word of physical tiredness induced by work, exertion or heat. . . . The emphasis is on the great effort expended by one who labors unceasingly for the congregation's welfare.[1]

Finally we come to a word I often use to describe life. Paul talks about his teaching ministry as a STRUGGLE. In typical Pauline vocabulary, this term describes competition. It reminds us that there can be no laziness among Christ's teachers who carry out this process on His behalf. The old cliché rings true: no pain—no gain. If we don't get the point in verse 29, it comes at us again in the first verse of the next chapter where Paul writes, "I want you to know how much I am struggling for you."

But the process carries its bright moments as well. Those of us who teach children receive a special grace from God, not only to provide sufficient patience for the task, but also to enjoy the abundant humor it provides. Consider the following story published in *Reader's Digest* a few years ago.

> Every morning before starting her class, the teacher would write the date on the blackboard, and if it had any significance in history, she would add a comment. On October 12, she knew that simply writing "Columbus Day" would be an insult to her students' intelligence. Instead, she wrote, "It all started almost 500 years ago today." Then she went out into the hall to monitor students on the way to class. As the starting bell rang, she stepped back into the room—and was greeted by a chorus of 27 voices singing "Happy Birthday to you."[2]

Before we leave this section we need to say a word about one of the key concepts in our title since all this goes on "with all wisdom." When we live with wisdom, we live with an understanding of how to apply the knowledge God has given us to achieve the ends He has assigned us. One translation suggests this text should read "with all possible wisdom," reminding us that we can only bring to the task the kind of mental and spiritual equipment God has granted us. Perhaps this suggests that some problems in classroom teaching and educational administration may lie beyond the capabilities you and I might have at any given point in our careers.

OUR PURPOSE

If we could design a motto from these two verses to describe the central objective of Christian education, it might sound like this: *To present perfect people.* We do this presenting in the light of Christ's return since the entire chapter implies the future toward which Christians now work and walk. Throughout all his epistles Paul links the idea of perfection with the coming of the Lord. It may not be out of line here to think of our students as trophies which we present to Christ.

Think about all the roll books you have handled in your years of teaching. Someday we will present to the Savior a list of students who, because of our influence, have moved to a solid walk with God and an expectation of the Lord's return. To be sure, that list won't include every student we have taught, but by His grace there is a list and the people named there represent our admonishing, teaching, laboring and struggling.

I received a letter recently from a young woman who served as my teaching assistant during my years on the faculty at Trinity Evangelical Divinity School. She now leads as a veteran missionary with her husband in a very needy area of the world. Their mission had just appointed her to a special council and she wrote to tell me about it. She indicated in the letter that she could not have possibly accepted this demanding appointment had I not pushed her beyond what she thought she could do during her years as a graduate student. In her own words, "You believed in me before I believed in myself." Every experienced teacher can tell such stories.

But we present these trophies PERFECT. You know, of course, that word does not mean without sin or fault. It typically describes a mature and complete person. Consider Murray Harris on this point.

> In Pauline usage *teleios* does not describe a person initiated into mystic rites . . . but rather a person mature in faith (cf. *v.* 23a) and in the knowledge of God's will (cf. *v.* 9c), someone who has obtained mature adulthood . . . and is no longer misled by false doctrine.[3]

The third word in our little motto is PEOPLE—we present perfect people. One emphasis in these verses does not show up, even in the NIV. Three times in two short verses Paul used the word "everyone." Admonish *everyone,* teach *everyone,* and present *everyone* perfect in Christ. Not the whole world, but the group of people for whom God has given us responsibility. In any given school year then, "everyone" means *every member of your class.*

I can almost hear the hesitation and see the shaking head as you say, "Impossible! You simply haven't seen my class." No, nor have you seen mine. But we cannot deny the emphasis of these verses. The point seems both simple and significant: every born-again student has the potential to become what God wants him or her to become. One may reject that option. Another may repel all our efforts at spiritual formation. But opposition and difficulty should never deter us from the purpose. *There must be no intellectual or economic exclusiveness in the Christian school and there must be no teacher who views a student or group of students as beyond the impact of God's grace and power.*

Paul had learned this the hard way. Early in his career he abandoned a young man by the name of John Mark as useless and immature, completely unfit to accompany the missionary team on the second journey (Acts 15:37–38). Dogmatic in labeling Mark an incorrigible case, Paul broke fellowship with his dear friend Barnabas and split the missionary team just to censure Mark. Some ten years later Mark again entered public ministry serving as an assistant to Peter and writing the second book of the New Testament. He became a Christian leader of whom Paul could write to Timothy, "Get Mark and bring him with you, because he is helpful to me in my ministry" (2 Timothy 4:11). Where are your Marks? How long will it take to equip them for effective life and ministry?

After Dr. Donald Campbell had served Dallas Seminary for five years as its president, he addressed the student body in chapel one day on the subject "Seven Things I Have Learned in Five Years as President." Everything Campbell said that day applies to what you and I do in developing people for a life of service to Jesus Christ.

1. The leader cannot control everything.
2. The leader cannot fix everything.
3. The leader cannot explain everything.
4. The leader must be able to make decisions.
5. The leader cannot run a popularity contest.
6. The leader must surround himself with strong people.
7. The leader can accomplish much more if he doesn't care who gets the credit.

OUR POWER

Once again the Greek text offers us a concept which does not come through in English: the word "energy" appears twice, once in verb form and the other a noun. One could translate this phrase, "Struggling in reliance upon His energy which energizes me in power." The word essentially describes the power to work effectively, something every one of us needs every day. Again the key verb (energizes) takes the present tense meaning that God does this for us all the time. According to O'Brien this text informs us that "the supply corresponds to the riches of the divine attribute and is more than adequate for the needs."[4]

So the labor and struggle are not up to us. Rather than being independent professionals holding legitimate credentials which certify our competence to do what we do, we are dependent servants, commissioned by the Master to present perfect people through the process of Christian teaching. Murray Harris offers an interesting expanded paraphrase of our passage.

> And this is the Christ we proclaim when we warn every unbeliever and teach every believer with all possible wisdom, our aim being to present every believer mature and perfect as a member of Christ's body who is in personal union with Christ. In my eager desire to achieve all of this, I toil and earnestly strive, energized by the power of the indwelling Christ that is so mightily at work in my life.[5]

Paraphrased even one more time into the ministry of Christian teaching, the passage might sound like this:

> Christian teachers proclaim Christ in their classrooms as servants of His body, the church. They admonish, they teach, they labor and they struggle in order to present perfect people to the One who has commissioned them for their tasks. To make possible what they achieve, He energizes them by His power so they may realize their eternal goals.

ENDNOTES

1. Peter T. O'Brien, "Colossians and Philemon," *Word Biblical Commentary*, vol. 44 (Waco: Word Books, 1982), 90.
2. "Quotes," *Readers Digest*, October 1988, 81.
3. Murray Harris, *Exegetical Guide to the Greek New Testament* (Grand Rapids: Eerdmans, 1991), 73.
4. O'Brien, "Colossians," 91.
5. Harris, *Exegetical Guide*, 75.

CHAPTER SIXTEEN

TAKING HEED TO THE WORD

1993

> BETH.
>
> 9 Wherewithal shall a you
> man cleanse his way? by taking
> heed *thereto* according to thy sh
> word.
> 10 With my whole heart have I
> thee: O let me not wa

Psalm 119:9-16

According to George Barna's 1991 book *What Americans Believe*, in a typical week just under half of all adults read the Bible. During that same week, one out of every eight adults who call themselves Christians reads the Bible every day. Interestingly, the likelihood of reading the Bible in that typical week increases with a person's age (61 percent for the over 65 age group and 32 percent for those aged 18–25). Furthermore, nearly half of all adults surveyed agreed that "the Bible is the written Word of God and is totally accurate in all it teaches."[1] However, this commitment correlated negatively with financial status. The more successful people are by worldly standards, the more they are likely to reject the Bible as God's Word. For example, twice as many people making over $60,000 a year disagreed that the Bible is God's Word than those making under $20,000. College graduates are three times more likely to reject that statement than people with a high school education or less.

All of which poses an interesting challenge and dilemma for Christian schools. We claim to teach the Bible as well as believe it as God's accurate Word. We also claim that study of Scripture enhances education rather than detracting from it. Those goals are encapsulated in this chapter's text, "Taking Heed to the Word," a phrase taken from the second section of Psalm 119. We'll place our focus on the action verbs related to God's Word.

David launches the psalm by offering a rhetorical question and then delivering its obvious answer: "Wherewithal shall a young man cleanse his way? by taking heed thereto according to thy word" (*v.* 9, KJV). We should not be thrown into skewing the psalm to a certain segment of the population because of the term "young man." David may very well have been applying this to himself or his sons, but obviously God intends us to see it without age or gender discrimination. Donald Williams observes about this verse, "The question is classic because it is the great issue of the Bible. How can a sinner stand in the presence of a Holy God? The cleansing of our way implies that we have fallen. How can we be washed and restored?"[2]

So right up front we are forced to apply a Biblical question to ourselves and to our common task. How can we and our students do what this verse demands? How can we take heed to God's Word?

By Seeking God

> I seek you with all my heart;
>> do not let me stray from your commands. (Psalm 119:10)

We are focusing on verbs in this study. I'll place each of them in the present tense since taking heed to the Word and learning about God through it forms a lifelong occupation. Our first point reminds us that Christians (and therefore Christian teachers) must worship God, not the Bible which tells us about God. Psalm 119 stresses objective revelation but it never describes the revealed Word as standing between God and His people. Instead, Scripture becomes the instrument to bring the two together. Since we know nothing about God apart from what Word and Spirit inform us, the psalmist makes sure every reference to Scripture in these verses aims us toward the Author.

"Christians (and therefore Christian teachers) must worship God, not the Bible which tells us about God."

Obviously this also emphasizes dependence, a very attractive posture for teachers. With the psalmist we cry, "Let me not wander from your commandments." In the words of Abraham Lincoln, "I believe the Bible is the best gift God has ever given to man. All the good from the Savior of the world is communicated to us through this Book."

But Lincoln died long ago and such talk is hardly the modern way of thinking. Today we live in what many call a "post-modern culture." Students from kindergarten through graduate school enter our schools with more baggage than ever before. Experiences have come to them second hand, rather like sitting in front of a television set watching a sunset scene while the sun sets outside.

Their culture has taught them to value speed over reflection, graphics over argument, marketing over principle, hardware over interpersonal relationships, and doing over being. Everything must be quicker, faster, further and sooner.

But seeking God takes time and somehow—in the harried, hassled world of education—we mentors must both demonstrate and communicate the process of seeking God. I like the words of David Schroeder:

> The world does not particularly need a greater number of highly-educated Christians. The world desperately needs a greater number of highly-motivated disciples. Today's classes of Christian students . . . represent a significant portion of the success of the next generation of Christians in carrying forward the work of the Kingdom of God and the Great Commission. Their success will largely depend on the willingness of today's Christian faculty members to become spiritual mentors. I encourage you as Christians, as disciples of Jesus Christ, and as faculty members to consider as part of your calling the spiritual nurture of your students.[3]

But, you may ask, what is a mentor? Simply defined, the word describes one who commits himself or herself to help another grow in some particular area of life—physical, social, intellectual, spiritual. Why not use the word "discipler"? Most experts agree that mentoring is a subset of discipling, a more narrow term. In my view, discipling more aptly describes what goes on in church or home and mentoring more appropriately defines what we as teachers do with students in an educational setting. But definitions aside, it focuses on seeking God—for us and for them.

Our students can only seek God as we both tell and show them how that essential quest takes place, a journey which begins in the pages of Scripture.

BY HIDING GOD'S WORD IN HEARTS

I have hidden your word in my heart
*   that I might not sin against you.* (Psalm 119:11)

Has any pastor or teacher ever handled this line without emphasizing Bible memorization? How interesting that we can narrow a text to one aspect of human behavior when its meaning seems obviously broader. A New Testament parallel I have commented on earlier would be using the last paragraph of Matthew exclusively in a foreign missions context.

Certainly our schools emphasize Bible memorization and surely that could be called hiding God's Word in one's heart. But what teacher has not watched students memorize pages of content in a mechanical and unresponsive way?

This text emphasizes being controlled by what we know the Bible says. In other words, the "hiding" process results in an active avoidance of sin. Christian teachers, modeling this behavior, should find themselves far more aware of their own sinful tendencies as the light of God's word illuminates the darkness of our hearts. Scripture clearly teaches that we will never be *sinless*; but we trust that the increased awareness will give us the grace to choose obedience and *sin less*.

Let me offer a caution based on the word "hiding" while publicly affirming this as a sidebar idea, not the intent of the text. Might it be possible that teachers in Christian schools can hide God's Word in a negative way? Hide its meaning and power from their students, perhaps even while intending to do just the reverse? Consider the following traps:

1. Lack of preparation for teaching a Bible class causing a failure to appropriately integrate Scripture with other subject matter.

2. Confusion about the meaning of a text or inability to explain a crucial point of application.

3. Unwarranted dogmatism on a given doctrine or interpretation. How quickly we lose sight of the fact that handling an infallible Bible does not guarantee us an infallible interpretation of that Bible.

4. Overemphasis on the cognitive domain. We come back again to the intellectual idolatry mentioned before. Quite frankly, Christian schools face a problem here. Academically oriented, driven by test scores and national norms, we forget that *affective* and *conative* domains are probably more important with respect to Scripture than the *cognitive*. What is the benefit in memorizing all the data in a doctrine class if our students develop a careless distaste for God's Word and an emphasis on orthodoxy over orthopraxy?

BY LEARNING GOD'S LAWS

Praise be to you, O Lord;
  teach me your decrees.
With my lips I recount
  all the laws that come from your mouth."
(Psalm 119:12–13)

True, the word "learning" does not appear in either of these verses, but the word "teach" does, and verse 13 notes that the student repeats what he has learned. Obviously the attitude of blessing God and the ability to communicate in one's own terminology what God has said form major goals in Christian school education. In fact, we dare say that the Bible creates the organizing principle of curriculum in the properly functioning Christian school. That foundational axiom carries through to the college level as well. Let me restate it. *Any school, at any level, worthy of the name "Christian," will so construct its curriculum that Biblical courses serve as the core of that curriculum and Biblical truth permeates its every part.*

Such a statement stands in total contrast to the current understanding of education on this continent. Perhaps you have read Neil Postman's description of modern education.

> In consideration of the disintegrative power of Technopoly, perhaps the most important contribution schools can make to the education of our youth is to give them a sense of coherence in their studies, a sense of purpose, meaning, and interconnectedness in what they learn. Modern secular education is failing not because it does not teach who Ginger Rogers, Norman Mailer, and a thousand other people are, but because it has no moral, social, or intellectual center. There is no set of ideas or attitudes that permeates all parts of the curriculum. The curriculum is not, in fact, a "course of study" at all but a meaningless hodgepodge of subjects. It does not even put forward a clear vision of what constitutes an educated person, unless it is a person who possesses "skills." In other words, a technocrat's ideal—a person with no commitment and no point of view but with plenty of marketable skills.[4]

Those words should frighten every Christian educator. We must structure clear-cut systems by which our students can learn God's decrees and laws, not just garner a hodgepodge of useless Biblical data. This is why I have so naggingly stressed learning beyond just the cognitive domain. We hope that many of our students will impact our non-Christian culture in a positive way as they build their families and professional lives. We may ensure failure with these goals if we don't teach a comprehensive Christian worldview that builds a foundation which facilitates godly decision making.

BY FOLLOWING GOD'S STATUTES

I rejoice in following your statutes
as one rejoices in great riches." (Psalm 119:14)

The theme of delight or rejoicing echoes throughout this psalm. In verse 14 we find the first such reference. It appears again in verse 16. Let's be careful to note that this is not the scholar's satisfaction, that moment of excitement when one discovers a useful piece of information to enhance class presentation or provide a poignant paragraph in a journal article. It is rather the disciple's delight and compared in this verse with "all riches." You and I could compare delight in Scripture with our wealth but, quite frankly, for teachers, that would not be saying much. But a king sitting in his royal palace while making such comparison offers a dramatic point.

Such rejoicing places us and our students under God's rule not through legalism and certainly not license, but liberty. This interesting link-up between law and liberty appears elsewhere in this psalm.

> *I run in the path of your commands,*
> > *for you have set my heart free.* (Psalm 119:32)
> *I will walk about in freedom,*
> > *for I have sought out your precepts.* (Psalm 119:45)

Such "nonsense" as finding freedom through voluntary obedience to God's truth is precisely the kind of insanity our alien culture expects from Christians. But society, not God's eternal truth has adopted convoluted thinking. Let me offer just one example—the use of the clock—and again I borrow a paragraph from Postman.

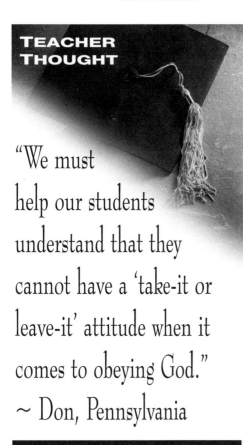

TEACHER THOUGHT

"We must help our students understand that they cannot have a 'take-it or leave-it' attitude when it comes to obeying God."
~ Don, Pennsylvania

The clock had its origin in the Benedictine monasteries of the twelfth and thirteenth centuries. The impetus behind the invention was to provide a more or less precise regularity to the routines of the monasteries, which required, among other things, seven periods of devotion during the course of the day. The bells of the monastery were to be rung to signal the canonical hours; the mechanical clock was the technology that could provide precision to these rituals of devotion. And indeed it did. But what the monks would not foresee was that the clock is a means not merely of keeping track of the hours but also of synchronizing and controlling the actions of men. And thus, by the middle of the fourteenth century, the clock had moved outside the walls of the monastery, and brought a new and precise regularity to the life of the workman and merchant. "The mechanical clock," as Lewis Mumford wrote, "made possible the idea of regular production, regular working hours and a standardized product." In short, without the clock capitalism would have been impossible. The paradox, the surprise, and the wonder are that the clock was invented by men who wanted to devote themselves more rigorously to God; it ended as the technology of greatest use to men who wished to devote themselves to the accumulation of money. In the eternal struggle between God and Mammon, the clock quite unpredictably favored the latter.[5]

BY MEDITATING ON GOD'S PRECEPTS

I meditate on your precepts
  and consider your ways. (Psalm 119:15)

This fascinating word meditation (which also appears in verses 23, 27, 48 and 78) can mean either loud emotion-filled speaking or quiet contemplation. It covers the gamut of spiritual reflection from strolling quietly through a garden reflecting on God's instruction or jumping up to sing, "Get all excited and tell everybody that Jesus Christ is King!" Surely the psalmist intends his readers to develop a familiarity with the text of Scripture, to know God's truth because they regularly handle and think about God's truth.

Clearly one of the major goals of teaching Scripture in Christian education is the internalization of truth; *we want our students to make the Bible their own* and live their lives in accordance with a personal embracing of God's Word. Søren Kierkegaard told numerous stories to illustrate his philosophy.

> It is related of a peasant who came (barefooted) to the Capital, and had made so much money that he could buy himself a pair of shoes and stockings and still have enough left over to get drunk on—it is related that as he was trying in his drunken state to find his way home, he lay down in the middle of the highway and fell asleep. Then along came a wagon, and the driver shouted to him to move or he would run over his legs. The drunken peasant awoke, looked at his legs, and since by reason of the shoes and stockings he didn't recognize them, he said to the driver, "Drive on, they are not my legs."

God forbid that any of our graduates awaken some months or years after they leave the school, look at their Bibles and say, "This is not God's truth."

BY DELIGHTING IN GOD'S DECREES

I delight in your decrees. (Psalm 119:16)

The word for "delight" here differs from verse 14 but the concept is the same. The word translated "decrees" in the NIV occurs twenty-one times in the Psalms, always in the plural, and literally means "things inscribed." In Isaiah 30:8 the prophet records the word of Jehovah: "Go now, write it on a tablet for them, inscribe it on a scroll, that for the days to come it may be an everlasting witness."

Philosophically, Christian education is committed to absolute truth. The National Endowment for the Humanities issued what it called "A Report on the State of Humanities in Higher Education," released in September of 1992 and entitled "Telling the Truth." Consider this paragraph from that report.

> The idea that there is no truth to pursue has a corollary: There are no standards to meet. What we think of as standards are, in the words of a law professor at the University of Virginia, the so-called "neutral" evaluative norms of the dominant cultural group. Educators, then, should not be concerned with A's and honors and other signs of excellence or even with the hard work and accomplishments that outstanding grades and high honors have traditionally recognized; instead, the goal should be political change, such as the creation of a society in which people do not compete with one another and everyone feels good about him- or herself.[6]

I'm quite prepared to argue that students should be less concerned with A's and honors, hard work and accomplishments, but hardly for the exchange offered above. I would rather trade those good and noble ends for *spiritual formation, knowledge of God's Word* and *involvement in ministry.* However, surely wise Christian school administrators, teachers and students can balance academic excellence and spiritual fervor, and that combination forms the ideal. Consequently, we could read the last phrase of our psalm as the tag end of anything we do.

"I will achieve the highest academic record I can in high school but I will not neglect your Word."

"I expect to take our basketball team to the state finals this year but I will not neglect your Word."

"I expect to lead our school's building program successfully but I will not neglect your Word."

"I will struggle and scratch to get through this first year of teaching but I will not neglect your Word."

Let's not get discouraged if all these noble goals have not yet been achieved. The psalmist describes a lifetime process, not something one achieves during a weekend seminar. If you have read any of Shel Silverstein's children's books you may have run across this poem entitled "Never."

> I've never roped a Brahma bull,
> I've never fought a duel,
> I've never crossed the desert
> On a lop-eared, swayback mule,
> I've never climbed an idol's nose
> To steal a cursed jewel.

I've never gone down with my ship
Into the bubblin' brine
I've never saved a lion's life
And then had him save mine,
Or screamed Ahoooo while
     swingin, through
The jungle on a vine.

I've never dealt draw poker
In a rowdy lumber camp,
Or got up at the count of nine
To beat the world's best champ,
I've never had my picture on
A six-cent postage stamp.

I've never scored a touchdown
On a ninety-nine yard run,
I've never winged six Daltons
With my dying brother's gun . . .
Or kissed Miz Jane, and rode my hoss
Into the setting sun.
Sometimes I just get so depressed
'Bout what I haven't done.

On March 1, 1991, ABC correspondent Linda Patillo reported from Kuwait on what Second Marine Division servicemen were doing that day while waiting to go home. She described them in these words: "They told war stories, they cleaned up, and they read their Bibles." If ABC should send Linda Patillo to your campus next week, may she be able to report, "They tell helpful stories, they live clean lives, and they take heed to God's Word."

ENDNOTES

1. George Barna, *What Americans Believe* (Ventura, Calif.: Regal Books, 1991), 286–287.

2. Donald M. Williams, *The Communicator's Commentary: Psalms 73–150* (Dallas: Word Books, 1989), 357.

3. David E. Schroeder, "Faculty as Mentors: Some Leading Thoughts for Reevaluating Our Role as Christian Educators," *Christian Education Journal* 13, no. 2 (1993): 38.

4. Neil Postman, *Technopoly: The Surrender of Culture to Technology* (1992): 186.

5. Postman, *Technopoly,* 15.

6. National Endowment for the Humanities, "A Report on the State of Humanities in Higher Education," *Telling the Truth* (September 1992).

CHAPTER SEVENTEEN

REMEMBER HOW THE LORD YOUR GOD LED YOU

fathers.
2 And thou shalt remember
all the way which the LORD thy br
God led thee these forty years of
the wilderness, to humble
and to prove thee.

Deuteronomy 8

In its twenty-fifth anniversary year, *Christian School Comment* reported the Association of Christian Schools International had experienced the largest growth ever over the previous twelve months.

> The combined student enrollment of the 3,174 member schools of ACSI has reached 661,475 this year giving us an increase of 95,940 students. This past year 35,228 teachers attended ACSI Teacher Conventions, an increase of 3,367 over the previous year! These figures are remarkable indicators of the Lord's rich blessing on Christian school education.[1]

To be sure evangelical schools represent a small percentage of "Protestant Miscellaneous" and "Protestant Miscellaneous" does not count for much of the total. Nevertheless our growth over the past two decades has been nothing short of phenomenal. By any statistic—number of member schools, number of teachers, attendance at conventions, achievement of graduates—God has richly and graciously blessed the Christian school movement in the last quarter of the twentieth century.

On the basis of that blessing we do well to heed the words of Moses recorded in Deuteronomy 8:10: "When you have eaten and are satisfied, praise the Lord your God for the good land he has given you." In point of fact, the entire eighth chapter of the book of Deuteronomy focuses on how we should act when we realize what God has done for us. It forms a marvelous Old Testament prelude to New Testament Christian hope.

Deuteronomy 8 impresses God's admonitions on the Israelites. True, they had heard most of them before. Moses reminds them how God both provided for His people and disciplined them during the prior forty years. From that experience the nation should have learned humility and dependence because forgetting the Lord and turning to other gods would result in destruction. In their hunger, He fed them with manna; in their thirst, He provided water, sometimes miraculously. Of particular familiarity in this first paragraph of our chapter (*vv.* 1–5) is verse 3, quoted by Jesus when tempted in the wilderness: "Man does not live on bread alone but on every word that comes from the mouth of the Lord."

GOD'S GRACE IN THE PAST

Be careful to follow every command I am giving you today, so that you may live and increase and may enter and possess the land that the Lord promised on oath to your forefathers. Remember how the Lord your God led you all the way in the desert these forty years, to humble you and to test you in order to know what was in your heart, whether or not you would keep his commands. He humbled you, causing you to hunger and then feeding you with manna, which neither you nor your fathers had known, to teach you that man does not live on bread alone but on every word that comes from the mouth of the Lord. Your clothes did not wear out and your feet did not swell during these forty years. Know then in your heart that as a man disciplines his son, so the Lord your God disciplines you. (Deuteronomy 8:1–5)

> "Christian educators understand that both Old Testament sacrifices and rituals as well as the historic experience of God's people represent a teaching model not only for them, but for us today."

Not so long ago, the Christian school movement, like Israel of old, wandered in the wilderness. I'm thinking particularly of the interdenominational wing. Some of us can remember when it would have been impossible in any major city to have a convention like those now held all over the continent each year. Not only would teacher interest have been insufficient, but the evangelical public would have thought it some kind of aberration rather than a movement of importance deserving support.

But even then God was leading, humbling us, causing us to hunger, and then feeding us with manna. Christian educators understand that both Old Testament sacrifices and rituals as well as the historic experience of God's people represent a teaching model not only for them, but for us today. One commentator picks up on the teaching tone of these verses.

> The purpose of these experiences was educational. Often in the Old Testament God is shown as sending suffering to humble and to discipline His servants so that they may learn lessons they would otherwise miss (e.g., the testing of Abraham, Job, Joseph, Jeremiah). God's methods have not changed over the centuries. The family of God still learns lessons through suffering.[2]

Out of these five verses alone come three essential concepts describing how God deals with us and perhaps, therefore, how we should deal with our students.

Devotion

God led His people to humble them, to test them and to know their hearts. We hear a great deal in our day about values clarification and values education. In a distinctly Christian axiology, the greatest value of all is a heart devoted to God and to His Son Jesus Christ. This value cannot be found in contemporary secular society no matter how moral or ethical a given environment.

Spiritual devotion gives substance to the educational prerogative of the home, the church, and the Christian school. It must be modeled in constant daily behavior by every one who carries the title "teacher." Jesus explained to the Pharisees that what comes out of the mouth is more important than what goes in. What comes out demonstrates the nature of the heart and such devotion reflects God's greatest concern.

> "In a distinctly Christian axiology, the greatest value of all is a heart devoted to God and to His Son Jesus Christ. This value cannot be found in contemporary secular society no matter how moral or ethical a given environment."

Dependence

The growth of a movement, like the proper growth of a child, has *stages of humbling and hungering*. In such times we see God's designed teaching situations. Note verse 3: "He humbled you, causing you to hunger and then feeding you with manna, which neither you nor your fathers had known, to teach you that man does not live on bread alone but on every word that comes from the mouth of the Lord."

The lesson strikes like an arrow amid our fund drives and public relations campaigns. Such manna may have enabled us to survive in the wilderness, but neither people nor schools can live on bread alone. The heart and core of what we do rests not in how we finance it, nor in how we announce it, but upon our dependence on the Word of the Lord.

Discipline

Do not pass lightly over verse 5 which sounds a bit like Hebrews 12 in its emphasis on discipline: "Know then in your heart that as a man disciplines his son, so the Lord your God disciplines you." How often we discuss among ourselves better approaches to classroom discipline with appropriate focus on our students. Above that, however, rests the reality of God's discipline in our own lives often brought about, as this passage affirms, through some kind of deprivation or suffering.

All of this reminds us again how absolutely connected home, church and school must be if we are to achieve God's best purposes in the lives of children and young people. Perhaps a reminder from the brilliant historian William Barclay can help us at this point. What he says about education among the Jews ought to still ring true in the Christian school movement.

In any examination of Jewish education it is essential to remember two things—first, that Jewish education was almost exclusively religious education; and second, that, at all periods of it, the centre is the home, and the responsibility of teaching the child is something that the parent cannot evade, if he is to satisfy the Law of God.[3]

A genuine acknowledgment of God's grace in the past requires memory. Scientists tell us that the human mind can store as many as six hundred memories a second in a lifetime of seventy-five years without the slightest strain. That works out to 1,419,120,000,000 memories! When memory becomes flabby, lack of mental exercise (more than advancing years) is usually the reason.[4] Use your memory—and don't forget the grace of God poured out upon us in the past.

> "Use your memory—and don't forget the grace of God poured out upon us in the past."

GOD'S GRACE IN THE PRESENT

Observe the commands of the Lord your God, walking in his ways and revering him. For the Lord your God is bringing you into a good land—a land with streams and pools of water, with springs flowing in the valleys and hills; a land with wheat and barley, vines and fig trees, pomegranates, olive oil and honey; a land where bread will not be scarce and you will lack nothing; a land where the rocks are iron and you can dig copper out of the hills. (Deuteronomy 8:6–9)

The Lord our God has brought us into a good land, a land with streams and pools, with springs, wheat and barley. Like the Israelites of old, some of us can remember the desert years, we recall the nomadic period of Christian school ministry when survival rather than success was the order of the day. After the Israelites crossed the Jordan, only Joshua and Caleb were available to remind the new generation of how it used to be—and that reminder was important.

The context of our passage reminds the new generation to keep the Lord's commandments, a warning which has already been introduced in Deuteronomy 6. Moses develops a contrast between the wilderness wanderings of the past forty years and the richness and fertility of the new land.

> "Those of us who have been called of God into this vocation celebrate God's grace on a day-to-day basis."

Perhaps one way to celebrate God's grace in the present would lead us to reflect on the esteem and dignity afforded teachers in Christian education. As James reminds us in the third chapter of his epistle, teaching is serious business. Those of us who have been called of God into this vocation celebrate God's grace on a day-to-day basis.

> "We talk much about the battle for the mind in Christian education, but the real battle is for the heart."

We are communicators and, 140 years after Samuel Morse flashed four words clicking in dots and dashes over a primitive electromagnetic telegraph and thereby opened the age of telecommunications, we still ask in wonder, "What hath God wrought?" Newspapers in those days referred to Morse's invention as "writing with lightening." We might do well to give increasing attention to the supernatural dimensions of Christian teaching.

We have already mentioned numbers of schools and teachers as a quantitative demonstration of God's grace in the past and in the present. Certainly the honor of God's call must always shine its light upon our daily ministry. Many, perhaps most Christian schools, can point to buildings, library holdings, equipment and numerous physical and property assets for which we must give credit to God's grace. Such tabulation is hardly out of line since that is precisely what Moses rehearses in our passage.

But above all the quantitative measures hovers the reality of why we exist. Either God is changing lives on our campuses or He is not. Either children and young people walk more closely in the steps of Jesus, or they do not. True, affective measures are more difficult to evaluate than cognitive concerns. But remember the measurement language of Deuteronomy 8:2: "Remember how the Lord your God led you . . . in order to know what was in your heart." We talk much about the battle for the mind in Christian education, but the real battle is for the heart.

Recently a Texas historian by the name of A. C. Greene uncovered a 1920 "friendship book" compiled by an eleven-year-old girl named Winnie. In it, Winnie had asked her fellow students to name favorite things. For example, favorite songs included "Till We Meet Again," "I'm Forever Blowing Bubbles," and "When You Come to the End of Perfect Day." Several students chose hymns such as "In the Sweet Bye and Bye" and "On a Hill Far Away." When asked about best friends, students and teacher voted unanimously that the best friends of all were father and mother.[5]

> "While thanking God for His grace in the past, we do well to claim its powerful work in the present."

But that was seventy-five years ago. Long before R-rated movies, cable television, MTV and a continental drift toward carnality and even barbarianism. While thanking God for His grace in the past, we do well to claim its powerful work in the present.

GOD'S GRACE IN THE FUTURE

When you have eaten and are satisfied, praise the Lord your God for the good land he has given you. Be careful that you do not forget the Lord your God, failing to observe his commands, his laws and his decrees that I am giving you this day. Otherwise when you eat and are satisfied, when you build fine houses and settle down, and when your herds and flocks grow large and your silver and gold increase and all you have is multiplied, then your heart will become proud and you will forget the Lord your God, who brought you out of Egypt, out of the land of slavery. He led you through the vast and dreadful desert, that thirsty and waterless land, with its venomous snakes and scorpions. He brought you water out of hard rock. He gave you manna to eat in the desert, something your fathers had never known, to humble and to test you so that in the end it might go well with you. You may say to yourself, "My power and the strength of my hands have produced this wealth for me." But remember the Lord your God, for it is he who gives you the ability to produce wealth, and so confirms his covenant, which he swore to your forefathers, as it is today.

If you ever forget the Lord your God and follow other gods and worship and bow down to them, I testify against you today that you will surely be destroyed. Like the nations the Lord destroyed before you, so you will be destroyed for not obeying the Lord your God. (Deuteronomy 8:10–20)

This portion of our chapter contains one of the longest sentences in Hebrew literature. In the original text it begins at verse 12 and runs on through verse 17. It offers stern warning to all who have moved from the wilderness to the Promised Land and enjoy all its fruits and streams. Like Israel, we might have a tendency to forget where we have been and what God has done to bring us to where we are. Dependence can turn to independence and worship to worldliness.

THE YEAR 1994

- The ACSI Headquarters was relocated to Colorado Springs, Colorado.

- Forty thousand Christian school students in the U.S. and Canada provided special school supply packets for forty thousand students in the former Soviet Union.

- The ACSI accreditation program received full recognition by the National Council for Private School Accreditation.

- Rev. Gene Garrick, esteemed Christian leader and ACSI board member, went to be with the Lord.

- Dr. Roy Lowrie, Jr., Christian school leader, author and past president of ACSI, was ushered into the Lord's presence.

REFLECTING ON THE HISTORY OF ACSI

These verses do not merely call us to remembrance, they rather specifically identify the kinds of behaviors which develop when people who have trusted God in needy times forget to trust Him in prosperous times.

Pride instead of Praise

Notice the repetition of the phrase "when you have eaten and are satisfied" in verses 10 and 12. The Christian school movement has eaten and, to a great measure, is satisfied. Of course there are still hundreds of struggling schools and thousands of underpaid teachers indicating some dissatisfied people. But of the movement, one could certainly say in the phraseology of verse 13, our "herds and flocks have grown large and our silver and gold have increased and all we have has been multiplied." The danger in such a situation? That we will turn to pride instead of praise. Verse 14 could not be more clear: "Then your heart will become proud and you will forget the Lord your God, Who brought you out of Egypt, out of the land of slavery."

> "Let us seek a balance between so much comfort that we forget our God, and so little comfort that we cannot continue our ministries."

Certainly we know also of dangers of constant deep dissatisfaction—if no relief is found, it may lead to depression. To put it another way, when we fail to praise God for what He has done and constantly look at our problems and deficiencies, the general depression which permeates so much of the American workplace can settle even on a Christian school. As always, let us seek a balance between so much comfort that we forget our God, and so little comfort that we cannot continue our ministries.

Complaints instead of Thanksgiving

The longer I serve positions of Christian leadership and particularly in various phases of Christian education, the more I tremble at the spirit of complaining which seems to plague our institutions at both faculty and student levels. A good bit of this, of course, has to do with perspective. Charles Kuralt, recently retired after a distinguished career at NBC News once noted, "Thanks to the interstate highway system, it is now possible to travel across the country from coast to coast without seeing anything." And it is possible to serve in a Christian school which God has blessed and prospered enormously and focus only upon what we do *not* have.

Our friends in the reformed camp emphasize what we have come to call covenant theology. Churches in this tradition have been heavily involved in Christian education long before many of us. Perhaps a spirit of complaining pervades some sectors of Christian education because we have not taken a serious enough view of what it means to be children of the covenant. Certainly it means recognizing that every desk, every inch of chalkboard space, every piece of teaching equipment—to say nothing of the privilege of our own educations—are all gifts of God's grace.

> "Every desk, every inch of chalkboard space, every piece of teaching equipment—to say nothing of the privilege of our own educations—are all gifts of God's grace."

Irresponsibility instead of Integrity

Integrity means being honest, complete and undivided. Integrity means doing what you say you will do, keeping your promises. That's what God expects from a people to whom He has given much. A people like us.

And among a people like us, one finds it difficult to imagine teachers and administrators who give in to irresponsibility, though surely they exist. Even apart from educational competence, our text warns us that it is irresponsible to say (or think), "My power and the strength of my hands have produced this [competence] for me" (v. 17).

The Bible calls us to responsibility, maturity and integrity. But integrity is far more than just signing a doctrinal statement or agreeing to abide by the rules of the school, imperfect though they may be. There are those in our society who want to purge every Christian institution of legalism, a noble goal. But without the boundaries of responsibility and integrity, one can behave in such a way as to dismantle the very school itself, treading on its traditions and scoffing at its scars.

All of us are to a certain extent the products of our age. Only a constant sensitivity to God's Spirit and faithfulness to His Word can deliver us from carrying the

> "Only a constant sensitivity to God's Spirit and faithfulness to His Word can deliver us from carrying the virus of a sinful society to our own campuses."

virus of a sinful society to our own campuses. We seem most likely to do that when we forget God's work in the past.

We teach in a decade unprecedented in the history of Christian school education. The remaining years of this century, I believe, contain opportunities and responsibilities far beyond those we have experienced before or can even appropriately conceive of in the present. Will we function as God's servants in times of prosperity? Only if we clearly maintain awareness of God's grace in the past and present. Only if we clearly understand the genuine distinctive of a Christian school and design ways for truth to impact students who are products of the modern age. And only if we effectively handle God's truth, and its profound applications to every contemporary problem.

> "Will we function as God's servants in times of prosperity?"

Like the ancient Israelites, we are called of God. If Hans Finzel is correct, "to respond to a call is to follow the most compelling of many options, regardless of cost." Let us remember how the Lord our God has led us.

ENDNOTES

1. Paul A. Kienel, "Basic Questions and Answers about Christian Schools," *Christian School Comment* 25, no. 7

2. A. A. Thompson, "Deuteronomy," *The Tyndale Old Testament Commentaries*, ed. D. J. Wiseman (Downer's Grove, Ill.: InterVarsity Press, 1974), 136.

3. William Barclay, *Education Ideals in the Ancient World* (Grand Rapids: Baker, 1974), 17.

4. *Resource* (Spring 1990): 1.

5. A. C. Greene, "1920 'Friend Ship' Book Lists Kids' 'Favorite' Things," *Dallas Morning News* (13 March 1994): A45.

CHAPTER EIGHTEEN

REACHING FORWARD TO THINGS AHEAD

this one thing I do, forgetting those things which are behind, and reaching forth unto those things which are before, I press toward the mark the prize of the high call

Philippians 3:12-14

In the United States, lawns occupy more land than any crop including wheat, corn or tobacco. In 1992–93, Americans spent $750 million on four hundred million pounds of grass seed. In any given year, homeowners use ten times more chemical pesticides per acre than do farmers. In the Western states, as much as 60 percent of available water is used for lawns. If all the acres of turf grass in the United States were pulled into one section, it would equal the size of the state of Pennsylvania.[1]

People give themselves and their money to what they value. People give their lives to what they see as significant goals which will improve or enhance their futures. Though the Bible may say, "Sufficient unto the day is the evil thereof," most North Americans spend great blocks of time, talent and treasure "reaching forward to things ahead."

The book of Philippians speaks of joy. True, strong themes of thanksgiving, exhortation to sound doctrine, and Christian unity flow throughout its four chapters, but virtually every respected commentator emphasizes joy. Somehow in the midst of the corruption of first-century Rome, these believers in the congregation formed so humbly by a business woman, a slave girl and a jailer (Acts 16) had discovered how to function vitally for Christ in an alien surrounding. Such is the state of Christian education in the middle of the last decade of the twentieth century. Dr. Ted Ward, speaking to the National

Association of Professors of Christian Education in 1991, outlined four major themes of the decade: increasing violence, institutional reformation, international realignment, and intercultural conflict. Within five years everyone of them had become very much a reality.

We form part of a huge national enterprise. More than one out of every four people in the United States participate in the educational process in some way. That includes sixty-five million Americans according to the National Center for Educational Statistics which announced its figures in January 1990.[2]

Before us lies a passage of challenge to every Christian teacher. Somehow our part in this vast continental enterprise called education must be unique. It must radiate with the awareness that God has called us to be different, to be His teachers, in His school system, in His world, in preparation for the coming of His Son.

> " ...God has called us to be different, to be His teachers, in His school system, in His world, in preparation for the coming of His Son."

CHOSEN TO TEACH

Not that I have already obtained all this, or have already been made perfect, but I press on to take hold of that for which Christ Jesus took hold of me. (Philippians 3:12)

Christian teachers of the 1990s function in a volatile atmosphere. The FBI reports that our chances of being victims of violence in America today are one in 132.[3] Millions of us live in daily fear of crime and violence. Yet our judicial system seems incapable of handling punishment. We know that the average murderer spends 1.8 years in prison and the average rapist, a mere sixty days.[4] Repeatedly in this book I have warned that our culture stands in danger of dominance by a society obsessed with rights rather than responsibility. Indeed, we regularly exhibit a bizarre infatuation to protect criminals and neglect victims.

A Duxbury, Mass., fireman savagely clubbed his wife, fracturing her skull, severing an ear and leaving her partially deaf. A judge decided the clubber had been temporarily insane and acquitted him. But the fire department fired him. Big mistake. David Frum reports in *Forbes* magazine that the clubber filed a complaint and seven years of litigation produced a ruling from the Massachusetts Commission Against Discrimination: the clubber was a victim of "handicap discrimination" because his aberrant behavior wasn't his fault. The commission ordered him rehired and paid $200,000 plus 12 percent interest for back pay and emotional distress (which he had a right not to suffer).

Chosen in Spite of Imperfection

So we live in a very imperfect world and in Christian honesty we recognize we are very imperfect people. In earlier verses Paul has been talking about the Resurrection; now he reminds us that we have not yet obtained or received that wonderful changed body and mind. Conversion is hardly the final goal; spiritual progress affords the constant imperative. The phraseology "have already been made perfect" appears only here in all of Paul's writing. As we have seen in an earlier chapter, "perfect" does not mean without sin or blemish; it simply means mature or complete. Paul looked ahead to the completion of his salvation since so many things around him defied his understanding. Worse yet, so many things *within* him confused his logical theology.

This verse describes us. We have begun to walk with the Lord, but we have hardly completed the journey. Our schools are not perfect because teachers and administrators still struggle with sin. We must resist any phraseology in public relations brochures or platform speeches which suggest perfection for any school or our collective movement.

Chosen to Achieve Jesus' Intent

But, no sooner had he reminded the Philippians that he was not yet complete, Paul hurries on to say, "but I press on to take hold of that for which Christ Jesus took hold of me." The heavenly Father chooses His Christian

THE YEAR 1995

- The new ACSI Headquarters was dedicated on July 30.

- Dr. Paul Kienel assumed his new role as president emeritus and founder of ACSI.

- The ACSI/SAT 9 Christian School Edition was introduced after three years of research and development.

- The first conference for MK teachers of Europe and Africa (MKEA) was held in Kandern, Germany.

- The first teacher resource materials published in the Russian language became available.

- The Rocky Mountain region was established.

REFLECTING ON THE HISTORY OF ACSI

teachers in spite of imperfection, but He also chooses them to achieve some intent which the Savior decides for their lives.

"Press on"—a Pauline athletic metaphor which the Macedonian recipients of this letter would understand. Pressing on to the eager pursuit of a definite goal. Surely reference to "that for which Christ Jesus took hold of me" must be initially applied to salvation. Paul acknowledged that Jesus grabbed hold of him and won't let him go.

> "Do we practice a vocation or an occupation? Has God definitively called you or have you taken a job which pays the rent until something better comes along?"

But, for our purposes, I also refer to God's choice of you as a teacher. You already know my opinions regarding Christian teachers and the call of God. Do we practice a vocation or an occupation? Has God definitively called you or have you taken a job which pays the rent until something better comes along?

This whole passage talks about living rightly in relation to eternity. Kierkegaard once put it this way: "One lives only once. If when death comes the life is well spent, that is, spent so that it is related rightly to eternity—then God be praised eternally. If not, then it is irremediable—one only lives once."[5]

Chosen to teach and chosen to achieve Jesus' intent. A life lived that way with respect to spiritual growth and vitality of service requires not only purpose but strategy. In these verses, Paul intends to tell us that he had every intention of implementing both.

CONCENTRATING ON TEACHING

Brothers, I do not consider myself yet to have taken hold of it. But one thing I do: Forgetting what is behind and straining toward what is ahead. (Philippians 3:13)

Once a week, weather permitting, I get together with three other men for three sets of tennis doubles. We change partners each set making a friendly outing rather than a match of vicious competitiveness. One of the players tends to lose more sets than he wins on a somewhat regular basis, and when he teams up with me each week I have a stock motto which by now I am sure he has tired of hearing: "Remember the key, Bill, concentration—concentration!"

We have already identified Paul's athletic metaphor—pressing toward the mark. In any kind of sport, an athlete must focus. In the NFL virtually every stadium poses a threat to the visiting offensive team, especially down near the end zone. Screaming crowds make it nearly impossible to hear the quarterback's count and linemen who don't watch the ball can easily jump off sides while wide receivers may be playing a guessing game if the play changes. Verse 13 reminds us to concentrate on the Christian life. What marks that kind of intense focus?

Humility

Paul has already told his readers he has not attained perfection and now he adds that he does not consider himself "yet to have taken hold of it." If Yogi Berra were writing this verse he might have said, "It ain't over until it's over." Do evaluations show you to be the best teacher in your school? Relax, you have not yet taken hold of it. Did your basketball team go undefeated? That's great, but you have not yet taken hold of it. Of all God's chosen servants, it seems to me that pastors and teachers must repeatedly emphasize their vulnerability, their roles as growing Christians who struggle with many of the same things their parishioners and students find troublesome. I emphasize that because parishioners and students tend to see, albeit falsely and foolishly, a kind of perfection in their pastors and teachers.

> "Concentration in Christian teaching begins with humility."

Satan tempts us with several ego curses of ministry—the independent self, the invincible self, the important self, and the imperial self. We need to respond like the pastor who keeps a plaque on his wall which says, "There is one God and you ain't he."

Concentration in Christian teaching begins with humility.

Singularity

One of the most popular phrases of Scripture appears in Philippians 3:13: "This one thing I do" (KJV). My long-time friend Howard Hendricks likes to say about this passage, "Most of us have to say, these twenty things I dabble in." When we recognize our shortcomings in humility perhaps we're ready to develop the kind of focus that this singularity requires. David Jeremiah writes:

> Such concentration does not come naturally. It must be developed through rigorous training and ceaseless effort. We focus our lives in this way, then the routine work of each day, the moments we spend in relaxation, even the trials and sufferings we experience, take on new meaning as they become a part of the all things which "work together for good" (Romans 8:28).[6]

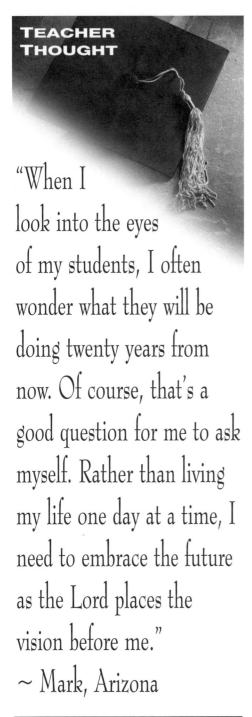

TEACHER THOUGHT

"When I look into the eyes of my students, I often wonder what they will be doing twenty years from now. Of course, that's a good question for me to ask myself. Rather than living my life one day at a time, I need to embrace the future as the Lord places the vision before me."
~ Mark, Arizona

What happens without focus? Our lives and minds become cluttered with a jumbled mass of unrelated facts and events. Let me slightly paraphrase a story from a book entitled *Mastering Worship*.

"Janie, when is Easter and what happens on it?" Janie said, "Well, Easter's in the fall, and we dress up in costumes and go trick-or-treating." Oh, no! the teacher thought. This really is a problem. Hoping for better results, he tried another student. "Jimmy, can you tell me when Easter is and what happens on that day?" Jimmy said, "Well, it's in the winter, and we put up the tree and decorate it and exchange gifts." Now the teacher was queasy, so he went to Mikey, the smartest kid in the class. "When is Easter, " he asked, "and what happens then?" Mikey answered, "Well, Easter is in the springtime when Jesus came up from the grave." "Very good!" the teacher said, relieved. Then Mikey added, "And if he sees his shadow, he goes back and we have six more weeks of winter."[7]

Now put this into an adult or young adult situation. Without focus, people hop aimlessly from circumstance to circumstance, just as these children aimlessly gathered facts without context, never really learning or making significant life change.

Memory

Paul is not talking here about obliterating the memory of the past. He merely intends that the mistakes and failures of the past do not impede our progress in the present toward the future. Was last year a horrible first year of teaching for you? Put it behind you and move on. Did the soccer team go 0 and 12 this fall? Maybe they will win one next year. On the one hand, we want to look back at the Lord's blessings as Samuel clearly emphasized when he reminded Israel that God had not brought them so far to abandon them. But human nature tends to dwell on past errors to such an extent that we are less likely to forgive ourselves than to receive forgiveness from God.

What did Paul put behind? Perhaps his Jewish heritage. Perhaps his years of persecuting Christians as a Pharisee. Perhaps previous Christian attainments. It matters not whether you are distracted by praise or public humility in the past—any kind of crowd noise can throw you off your game. I find it difficult to read this portion of our verse without remembering my own life verse: "However, I consider my life worth nothing to me, if only I may finish the race and complete the task the Lord Jesus has given me—the task of testifying to the gospel of God's grace" (Acts 20:24).

> "Human nature tends to dwell on past errors to such an extent that we are less likely to forgive ourselves than to receive forgiveness from God."

Intensity

Paul has already talked about pressing on, now he intends to strain toward what lies ahead. I like Robertson's description.

> It is the graphic word from the arena. The metaphor applies naturally to the tension of the runner in the foot race as he leans forward in his eagerness. . . . in sporting language he is on "the home stretch."[8]

But what lies ahead? In the strict context of the passage, our interpretation must focus on the Resurrection body and heaven. In the ministry of teaching, however, we never know "what lies ahead" and so straining to reach it always demonstrates a life of faith.

In 1947, a professor at the University of Chicago, Dr. Chandrasekhar, was scheduled to teach an advanced seminar in astrophysics. At the time, he was living in Wisconsin, doing research at the Yerkes astronomical observatory. He planned to commute twice a week for the class, even though it would be held during the harsh winter months. Registration for the seminar, however, fell far below expectations. Only two students signed up for the class. People expected Dr. Chandrasekhar to cancel, lest he waste his time. But for the sake of two students, he taught the class, commuting 100 miles round trip through back country roads in the dead of winter. His students, Chen Ning Yang and Tsung Dao Lee, did their homework. Ten years later, in 1957, they both won the Nobel prize for physics. So did Dr. Chandrasekhar in 1983. For effective teachers, there is no such thing as a small class.[9]

CHALLENGED TO TEACH

I press on toward the goal to win the prize for which God has called me heavenward in Christ Jesus. (Philippians 3:14)

Paul pressed on toward the goal which, in the racing metaphor, would be the tape at the end of the dash or distance run. In the spiritual application of the passage, surely Paul intends us to recognize complete knowledge of Christ which would only be attainable in its fullest form in heaven. But what is your goal? From weather forecasters to futurists, humans are notoriously deficient in predicting what lies ahead. Even the most casual remarks indicate the futility. I offer as an example the following pronouncements.

An MGM executive evaluating Fred Astaire in 1928: "Can't act. Can't sing. Balding. Can dance a little."

John Adams' assessment of Benjamin Franklin in 1779: "He has very moderate abilities."

The editor of the *San Francisco Examiner* in a letter in 1889: "I'm sorry, Mr. Kipling, but you just don't know how to use the English language."

Michael Todd's evaluation of an early screening of the Broadway musical *Oklahoma*: "No legs, no jokes, no chance."

> "However difficult the future at your school may appear at the present time, God may be naming you the point person who handles the pressure."

Goal Orientation

However difficult the future at your school may appear at the present time, God may be naming you the point person who handles the pressure. Larry Bird did not anchor the great Boston Celtics teams because of speed or height. He was the go-to guy in the crunch. Anybody can take the last shot when the score is tied, but only leaders want the ball when their team is down a point.

Prize Orientation

Can we see a difference between goal and prize in our passage? Probably not. Paul just pressed the connection between winning the race and getting the gold. The concept of goal fixes our attention on the race; the word "prize" pictures the celebration after the win. I hardly need to invest extra time telling Christian teachers that the prize for what we do may not be seen this side of heaven's gates. We all recognize that we do not teach for the money, nor do we get much recognition. But that does not keep us from being prize oriented as we wait to hear the words, "Well done."

Heaven Orientation

I cannot tell you how many times Satan tempts me with the thought that I have invested my life working so hard for so little material gain. I find it very difficult to rejoice that teachers are so widely heralded in Western society—and so little rewarded. But one could say the same for missionary evangelists like Paul and that is why both he and we "press on toward the goal to win the prize for which God has called [us] heavenward in Christ Jesus."

In short, if we don't keep the heavenly vision, we will be no earthly good. Christian growth demands much of us and so does Christian teaching. But the eagerness with which we reach forward to things ahead keeps us going as long as we realize that ultimate joy comes with the completion of God's work in our lives.

Assuming God has called you heavenward in eternal salvation, do you have a sufficient grasp of His call to teach? Do you know that He has chosen you for Christian teaching? Can you focus and concentrate on that ministry? Does the joy of what we do challenge you to the goal and the prize? The chapter, of course, does not conclude with verse 14. The phraseology of verse 15 sounds as dynamic in our day as when Paul wrote the words: "All of us who are mature should take such a view of things." Aboard the Enterprise we simply say, "Make it so."

Perhaps this study can best end by offering our passage from *The Message*, a modern language paraphrase by Eugene Peterson.

> I'm not saying that I have this altogether, that I have it made. But I am well on my way, reaching out for Christ, Who has so wondrously reached out for me. Friends, don't get me wrong: By no means do I count myself an expert in all of this, but I've got my eye on the goal, where God is beckoning us onward—to Jesus. I'm off and running, and I'm not turning back.
>
> So let's keep focused on that goal, those of us who want everything God has for us. If any of you have something else in mind, something less than total commitment, God will clear your blurred vision—you'll see it yet! Now that we are on the right track, let's stay on it.[10]

> "We all recognize that we do not teach for the money, nor do we get much recognition. But that does not keep us from being prize oriented as we wait to hear the words, 'Well done.'"

ENDNOTES

1. "The New Turf Wars," *Newsweek* (21 June 1993): 63.

2. National Center for Educational Statistics.

3. NBC News, 29 January 1994.

4. NBC News, 28 January 1994.

5. Martin E. Marty, "Context: A Commentary on the Interaction of Religion and Culture," *Claretian Publications* 21, no.8 (15 April 1989): 3.

6. David Jeremiah, *Turning Toward Joy* (Wheaton: Victor Books, 1992), 133.

7. Jack Hayford, John Killinger, and Howard Stevenson, *Mastering Worship* (Portland: Multnomah, 1990), 129.

8. A. T. Robertson, *Paul's Joy in Christ* (Nashville: Broadman), 111.

9. "To Illustrate Teaching," *Leadership* 12, no. 4 (Fall 1991): 44.

10. Eugene Peterson, *The Message* (Colorado Springs: NavPress, 1993), 416–417.